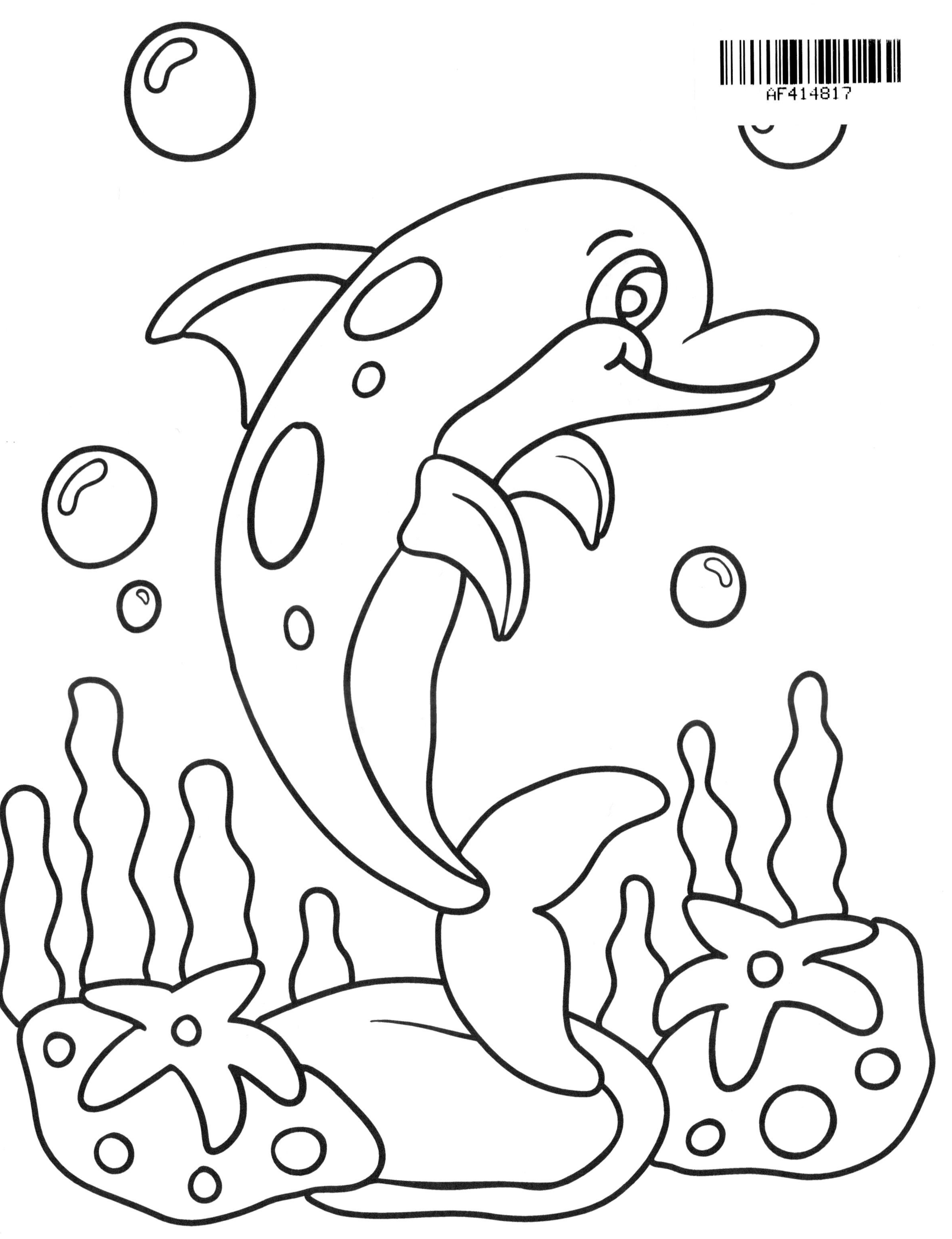

AF414817

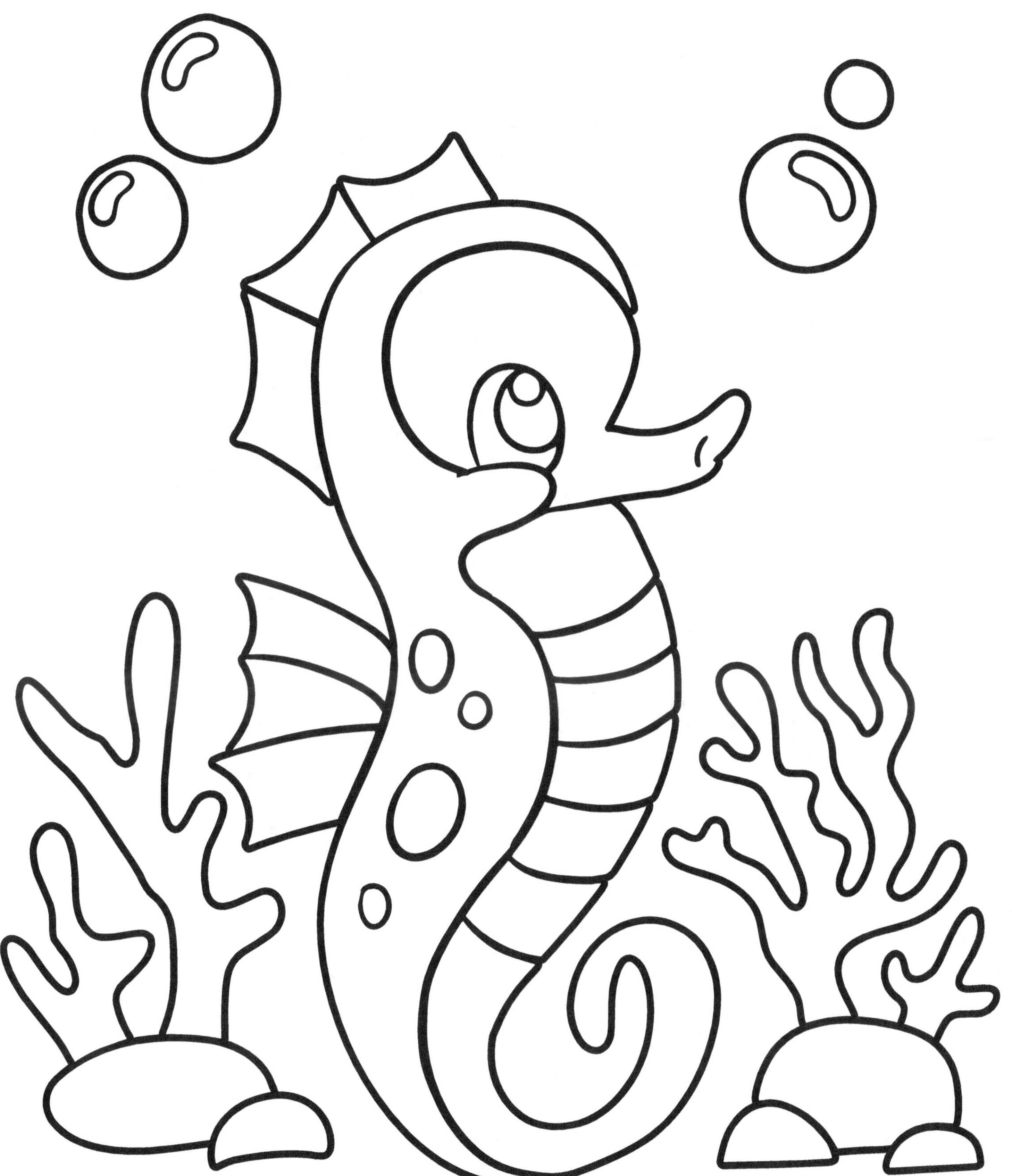

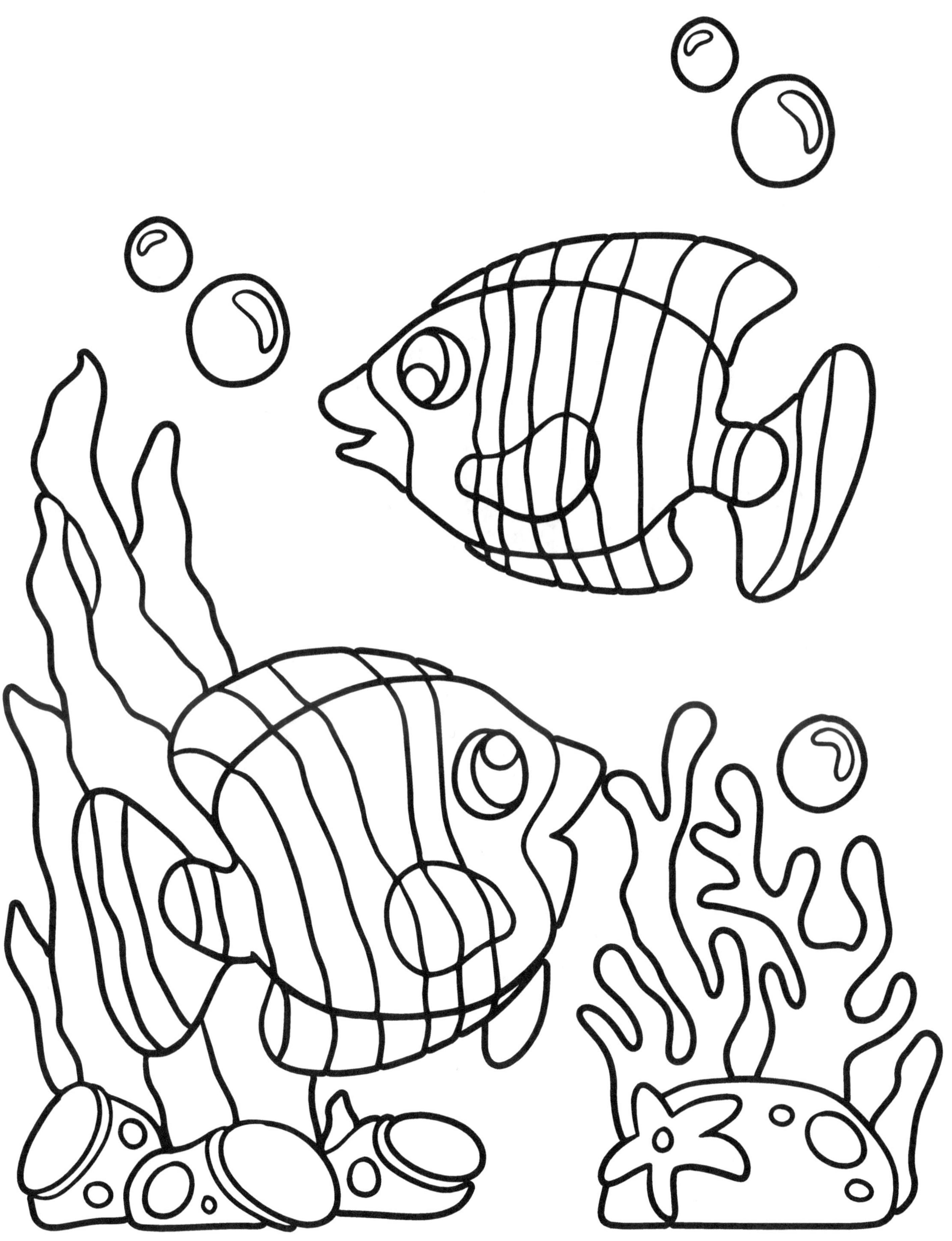

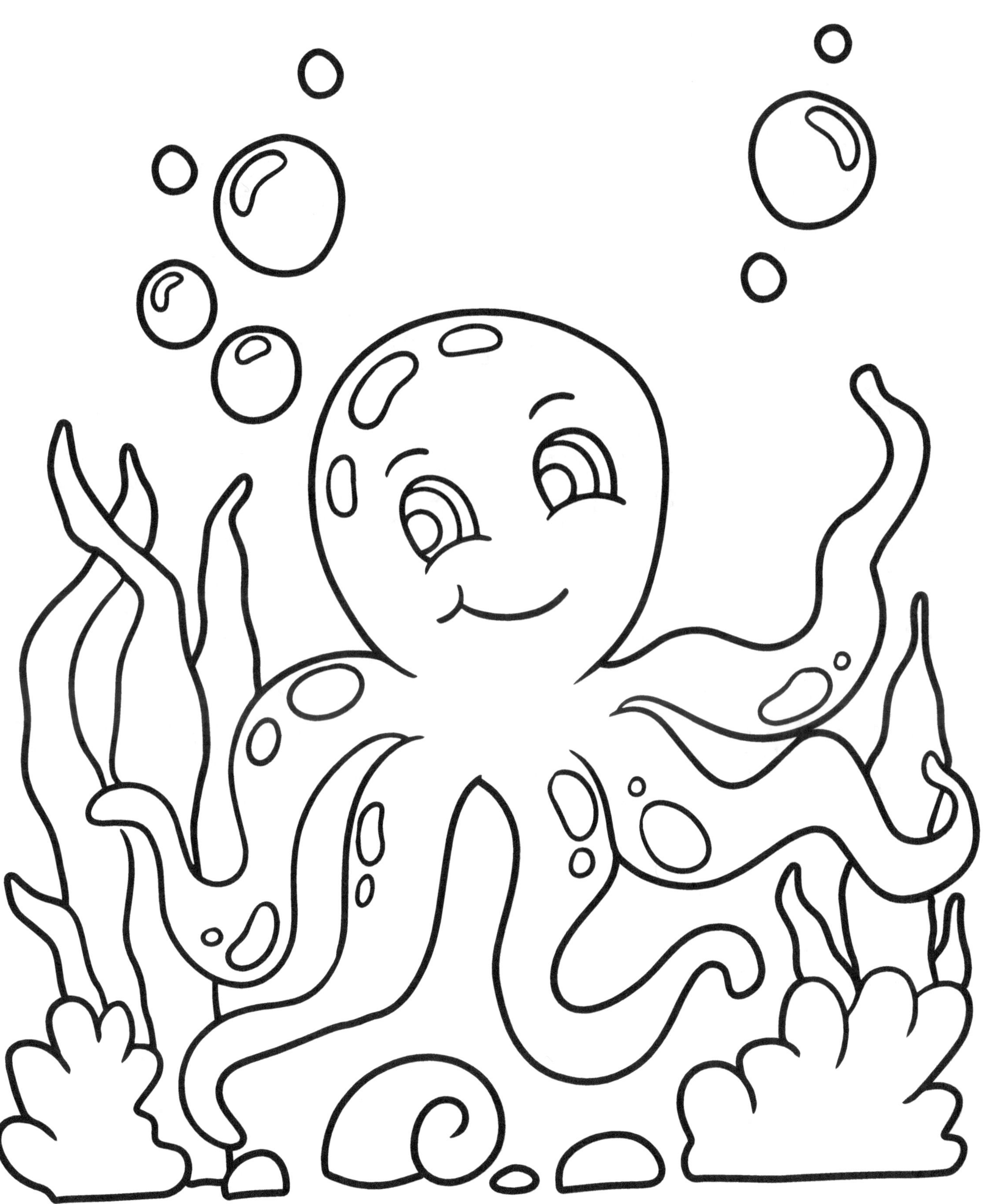

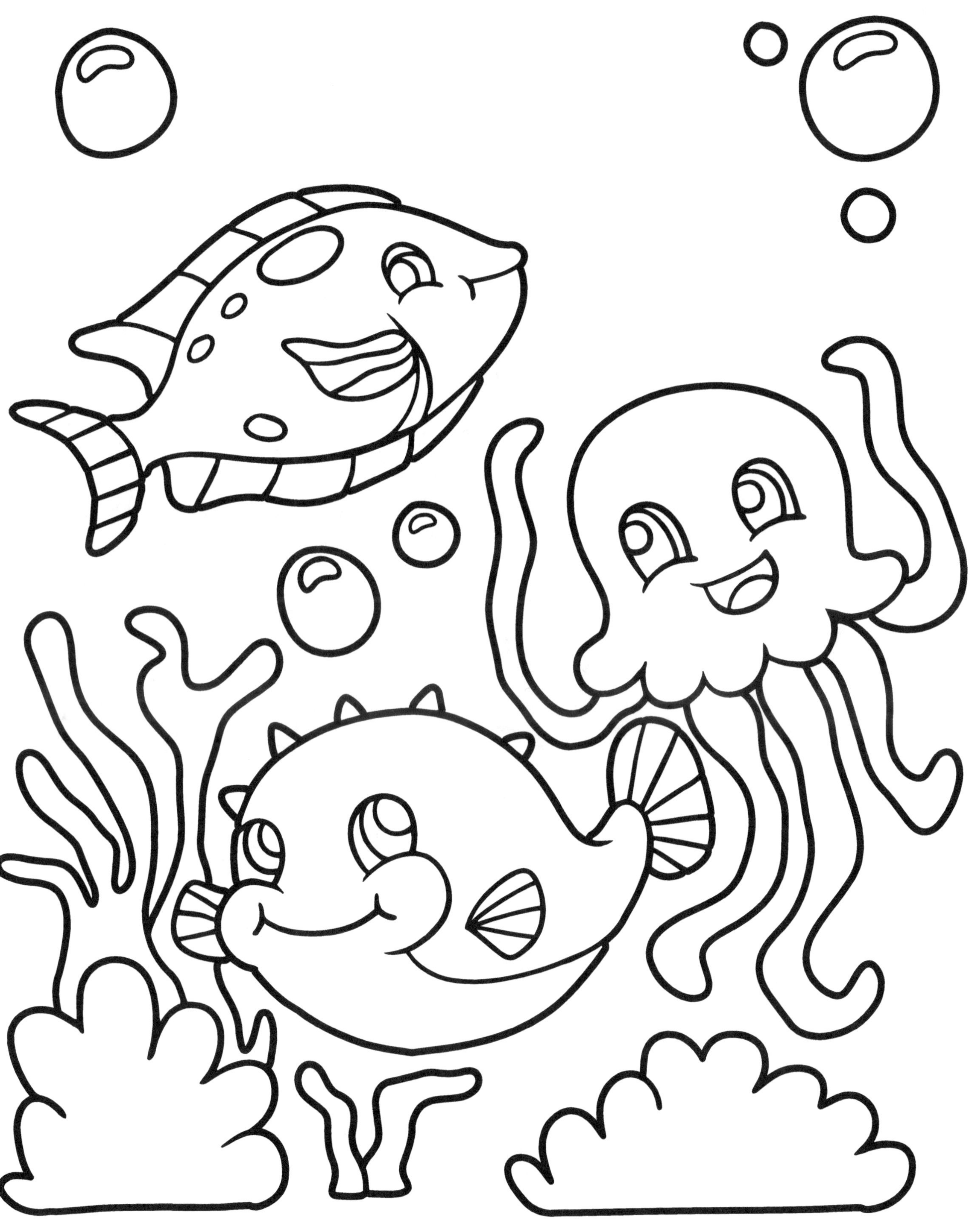

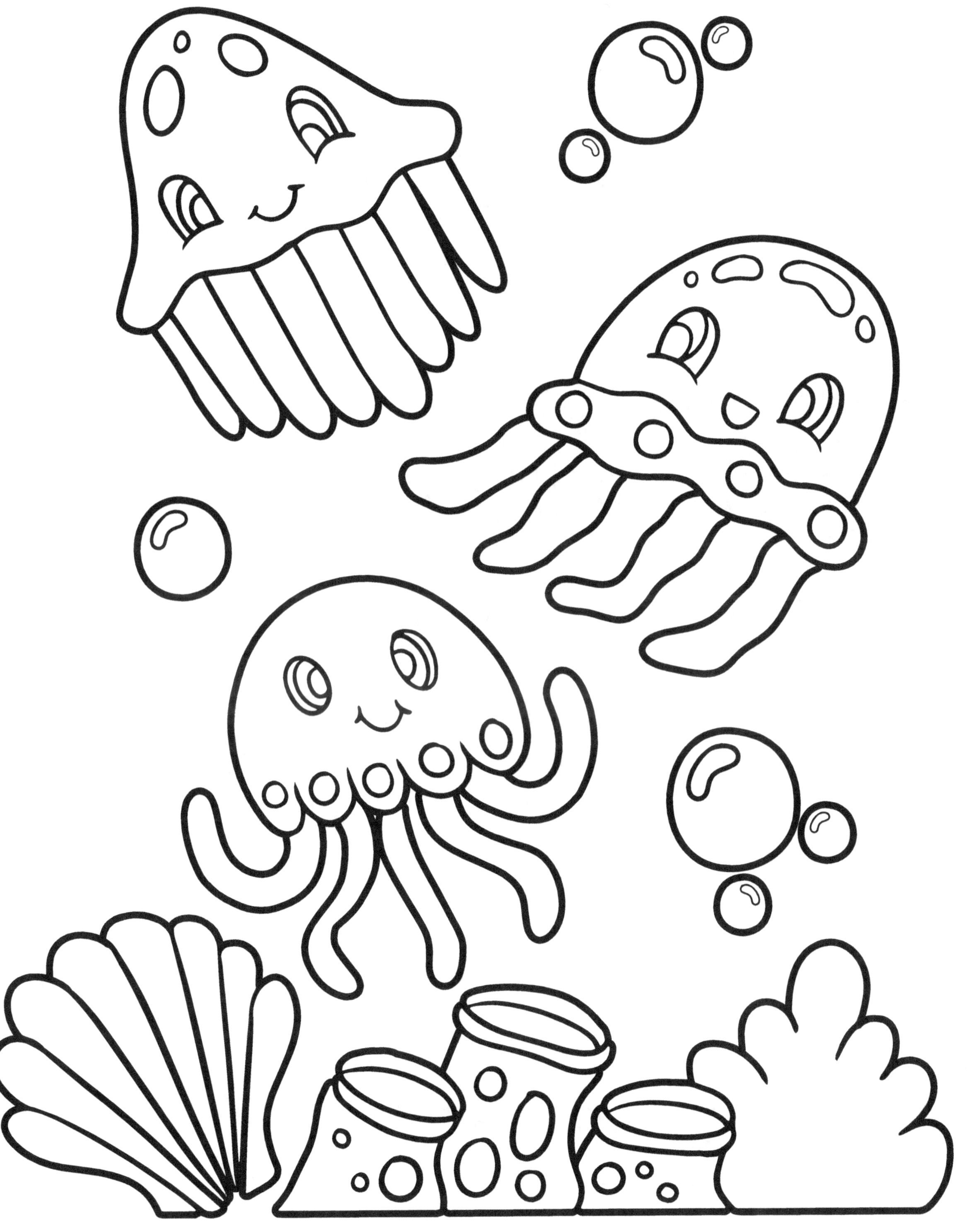

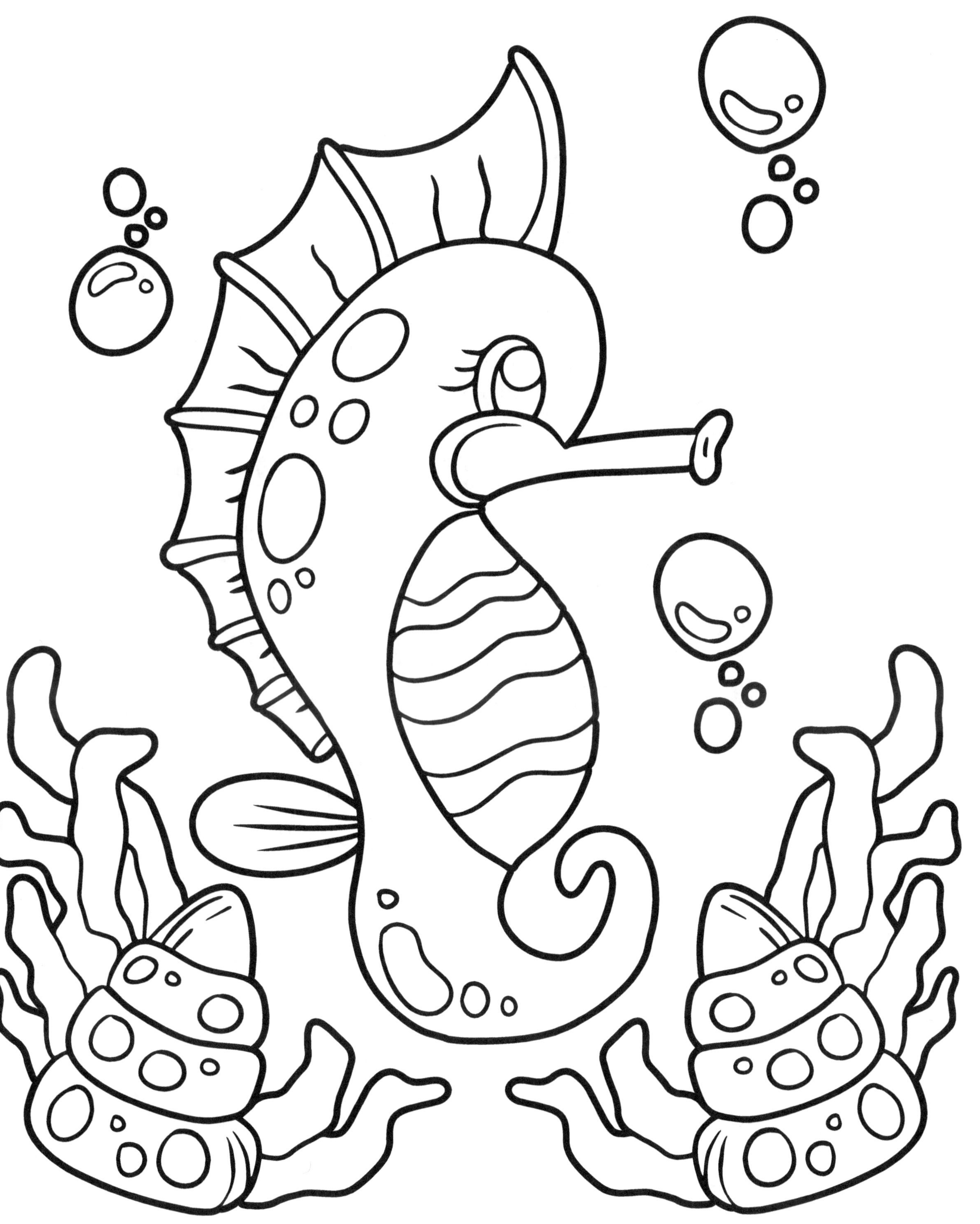

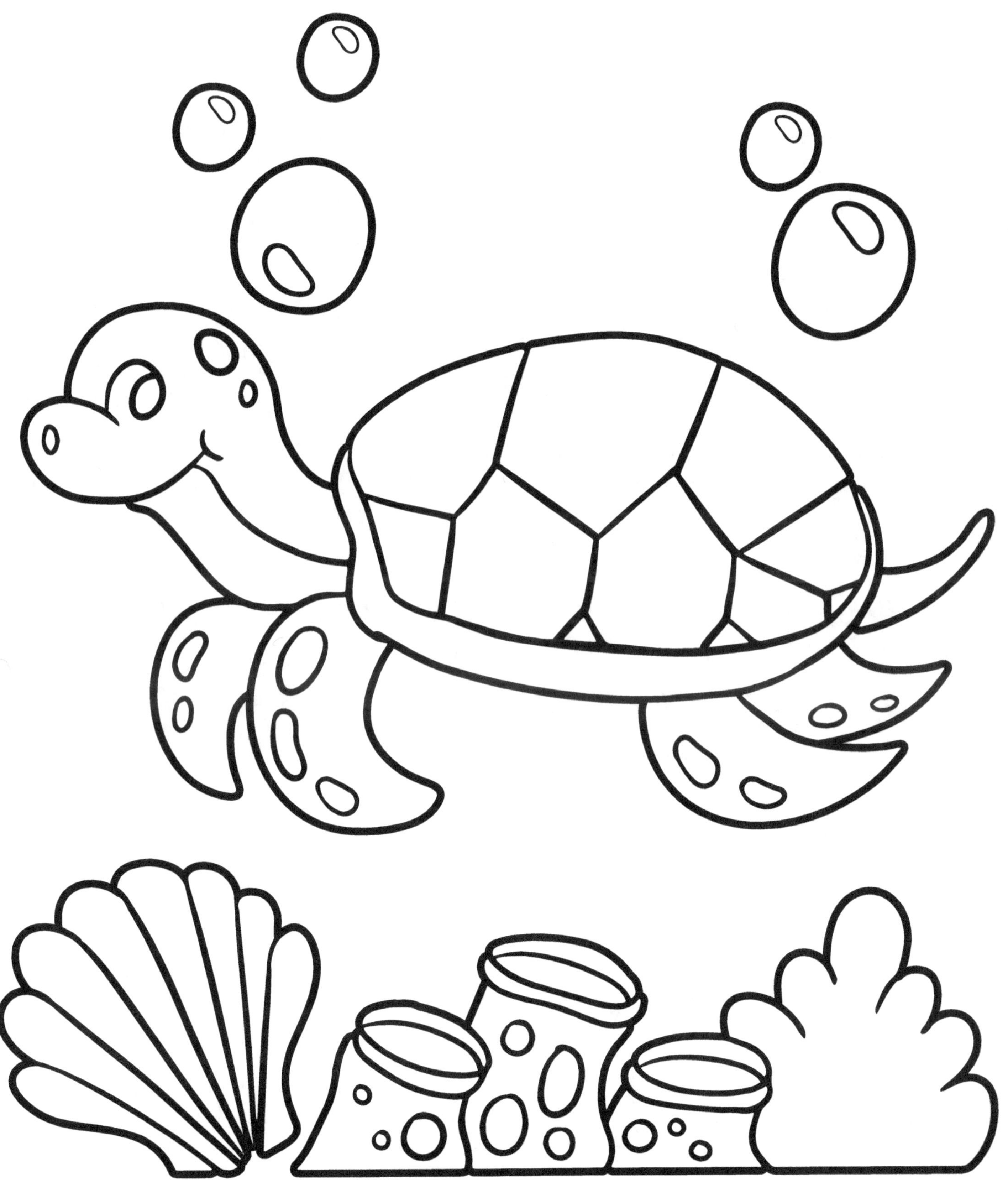

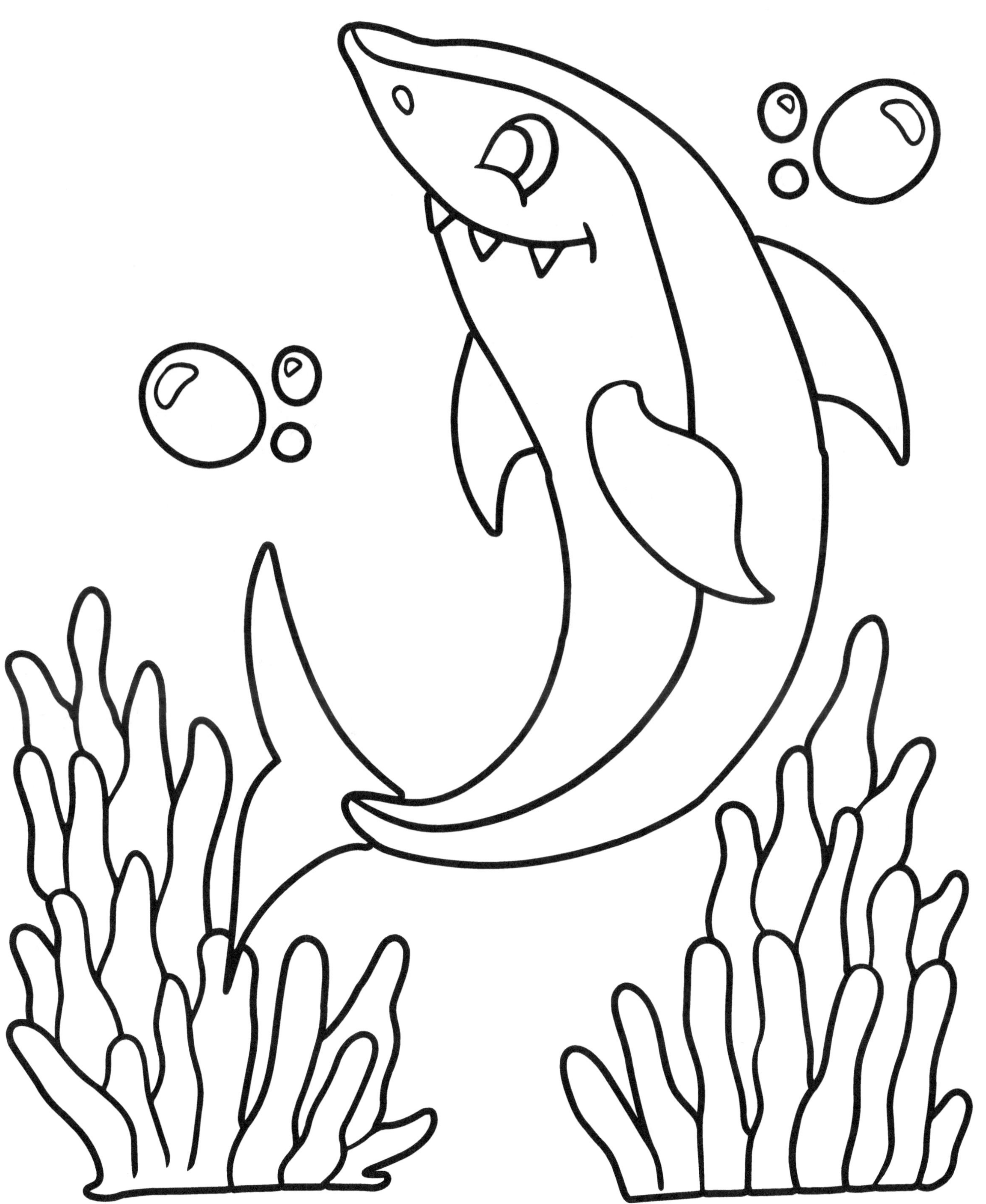

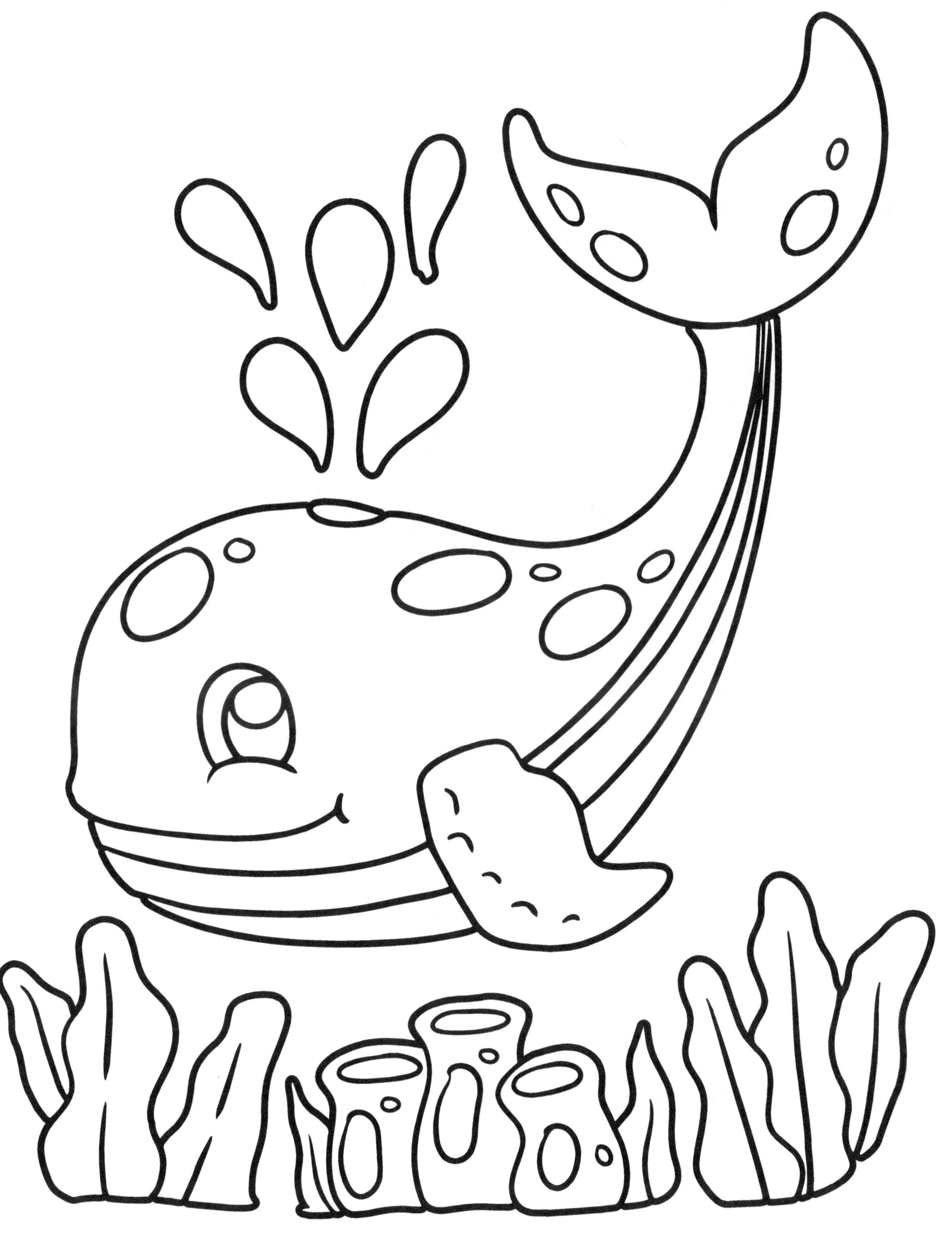

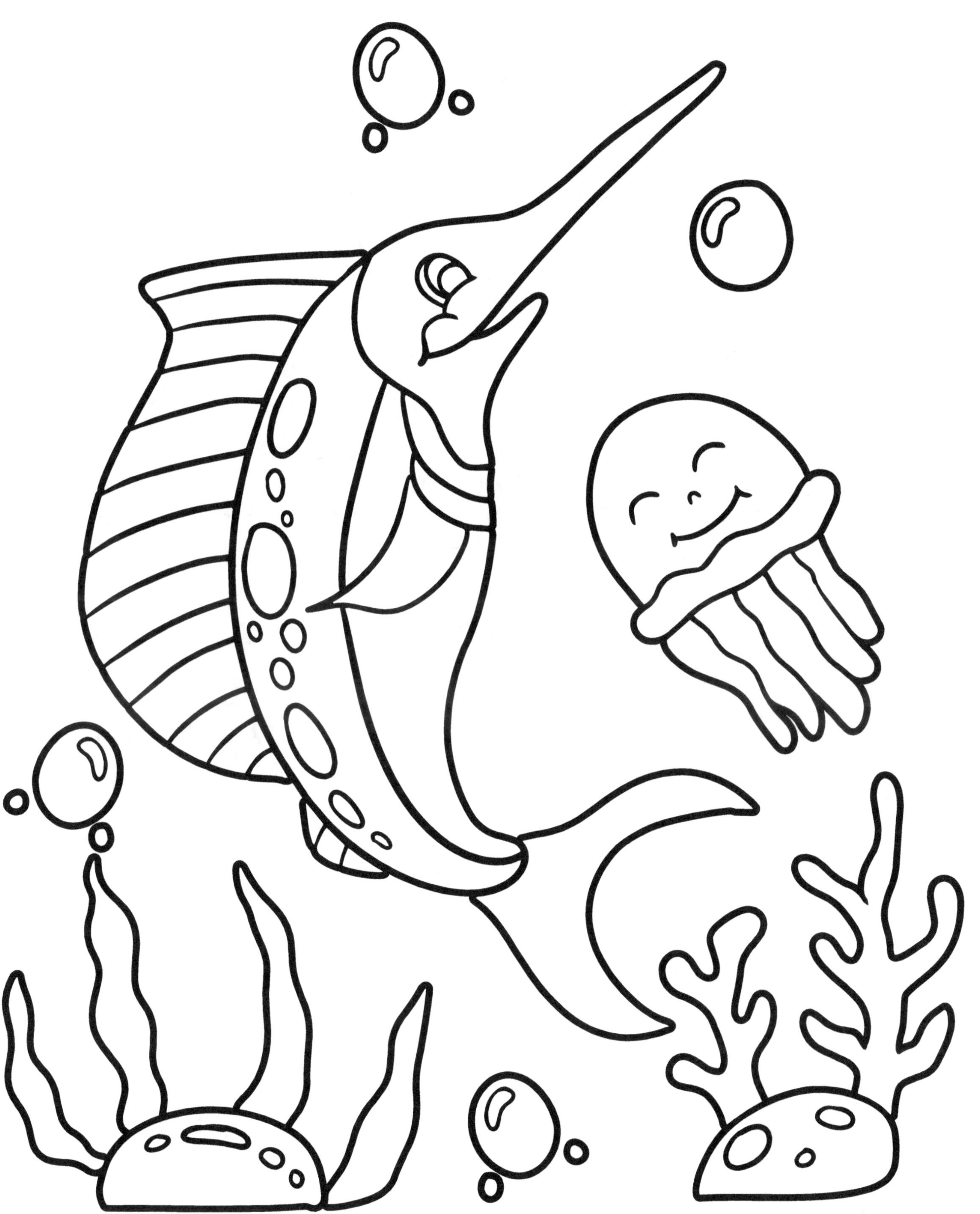

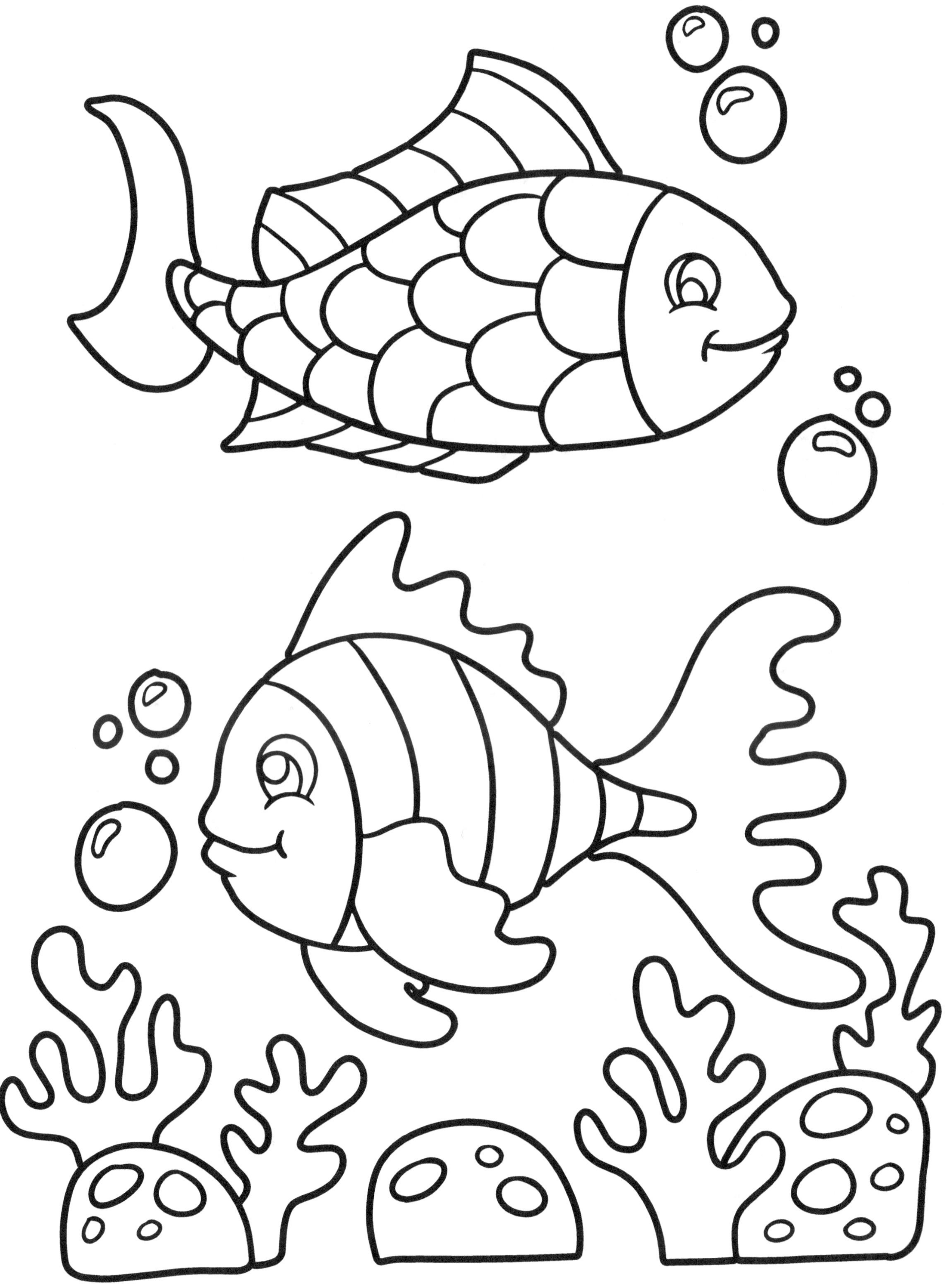

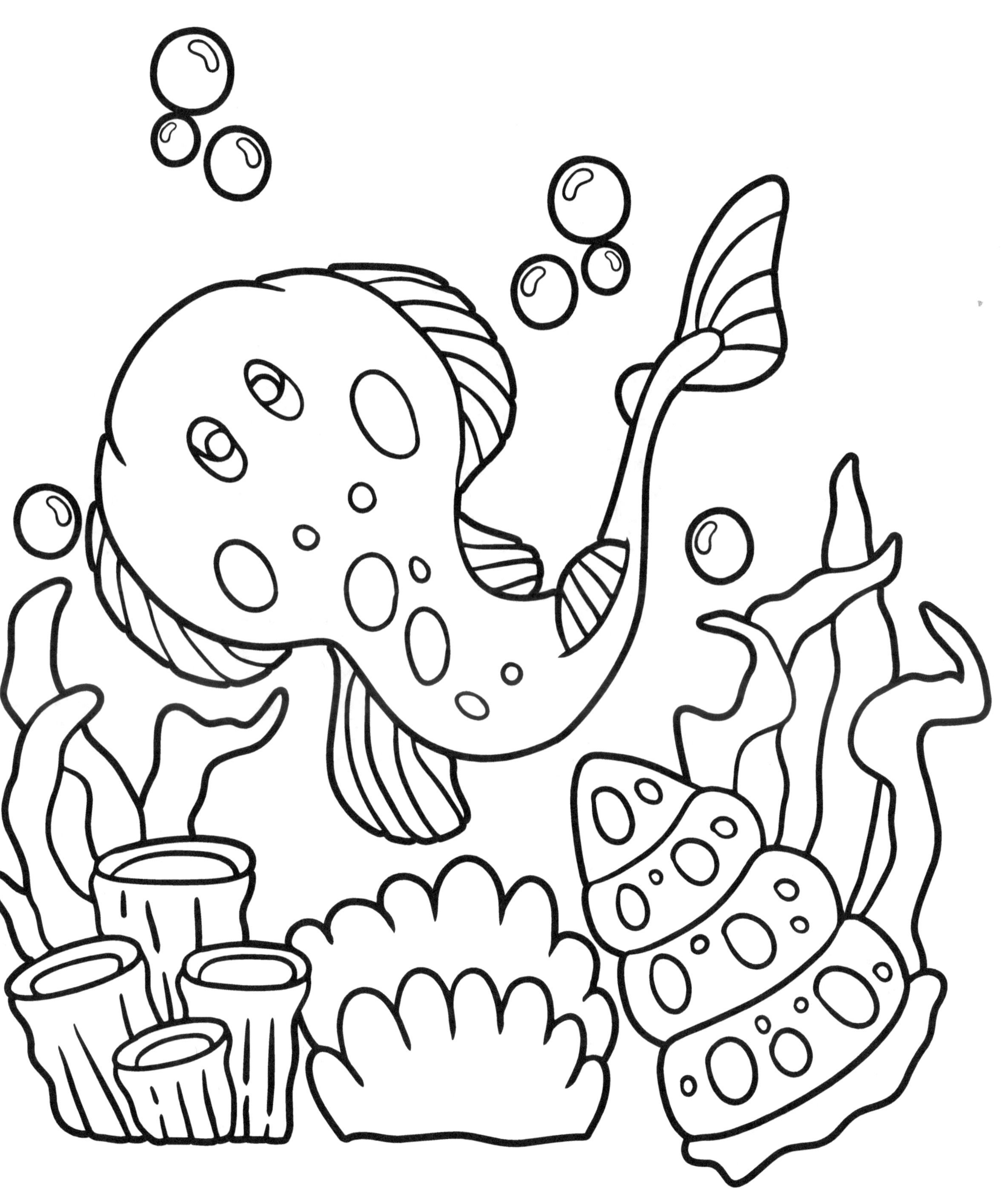

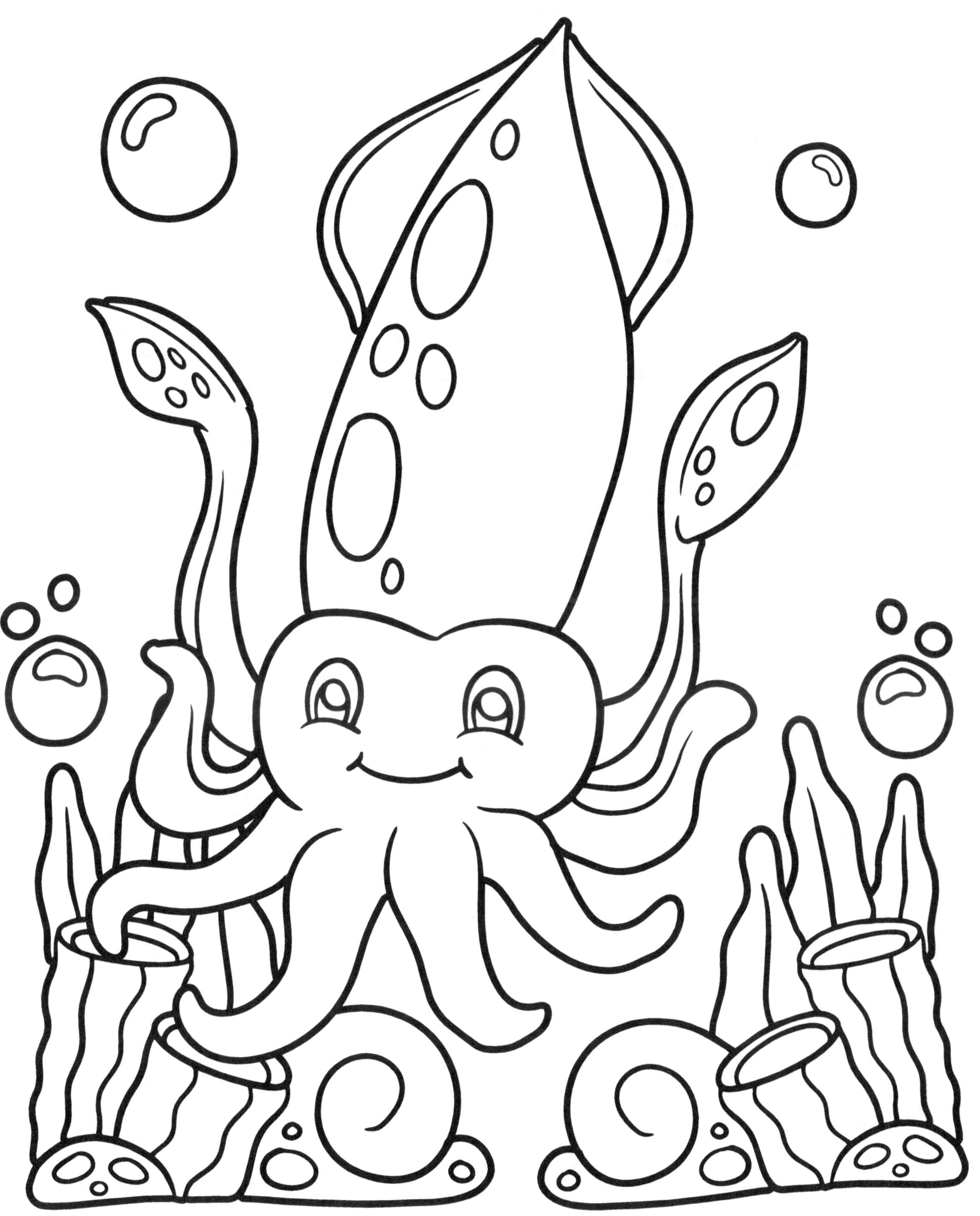

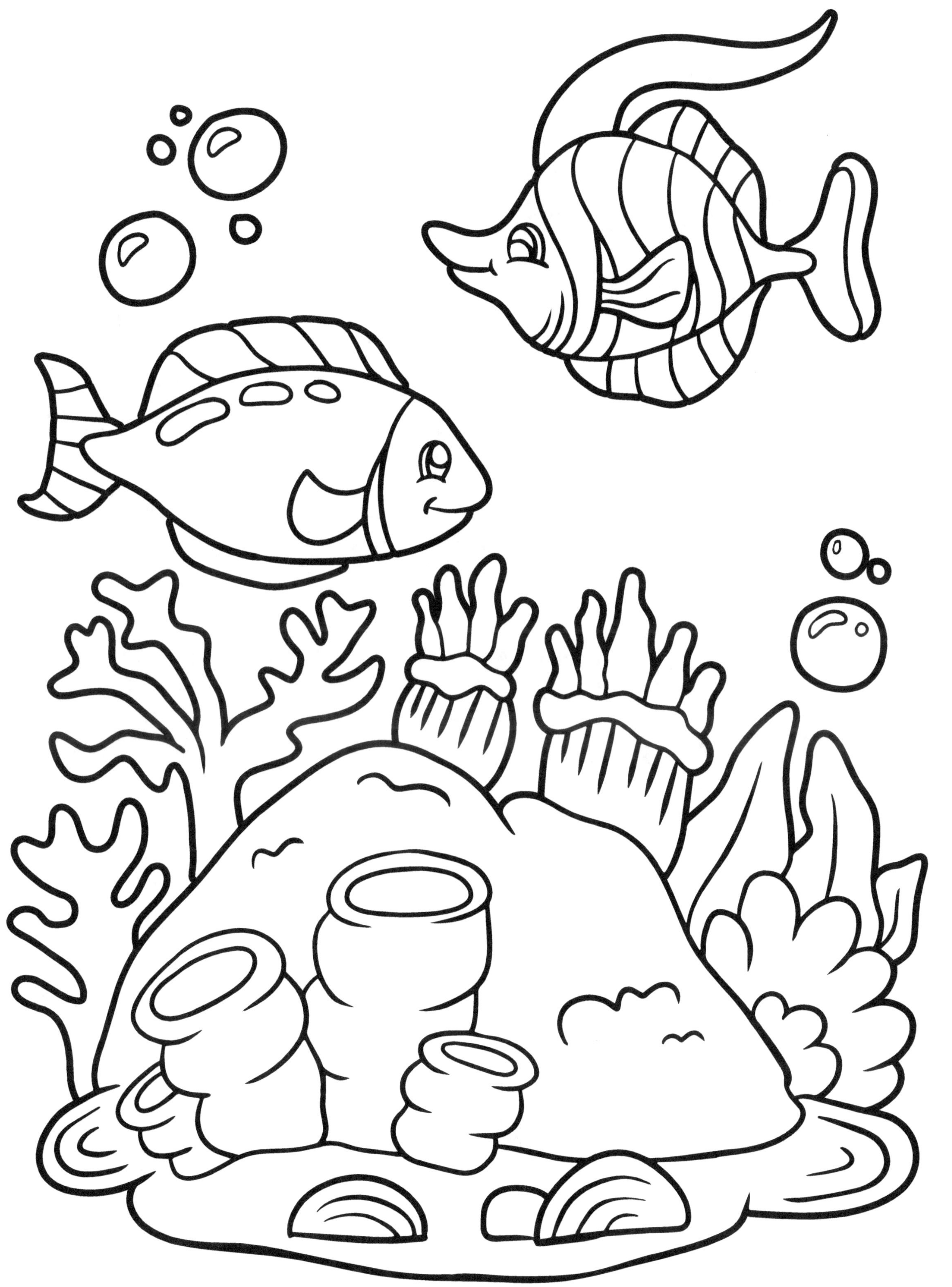

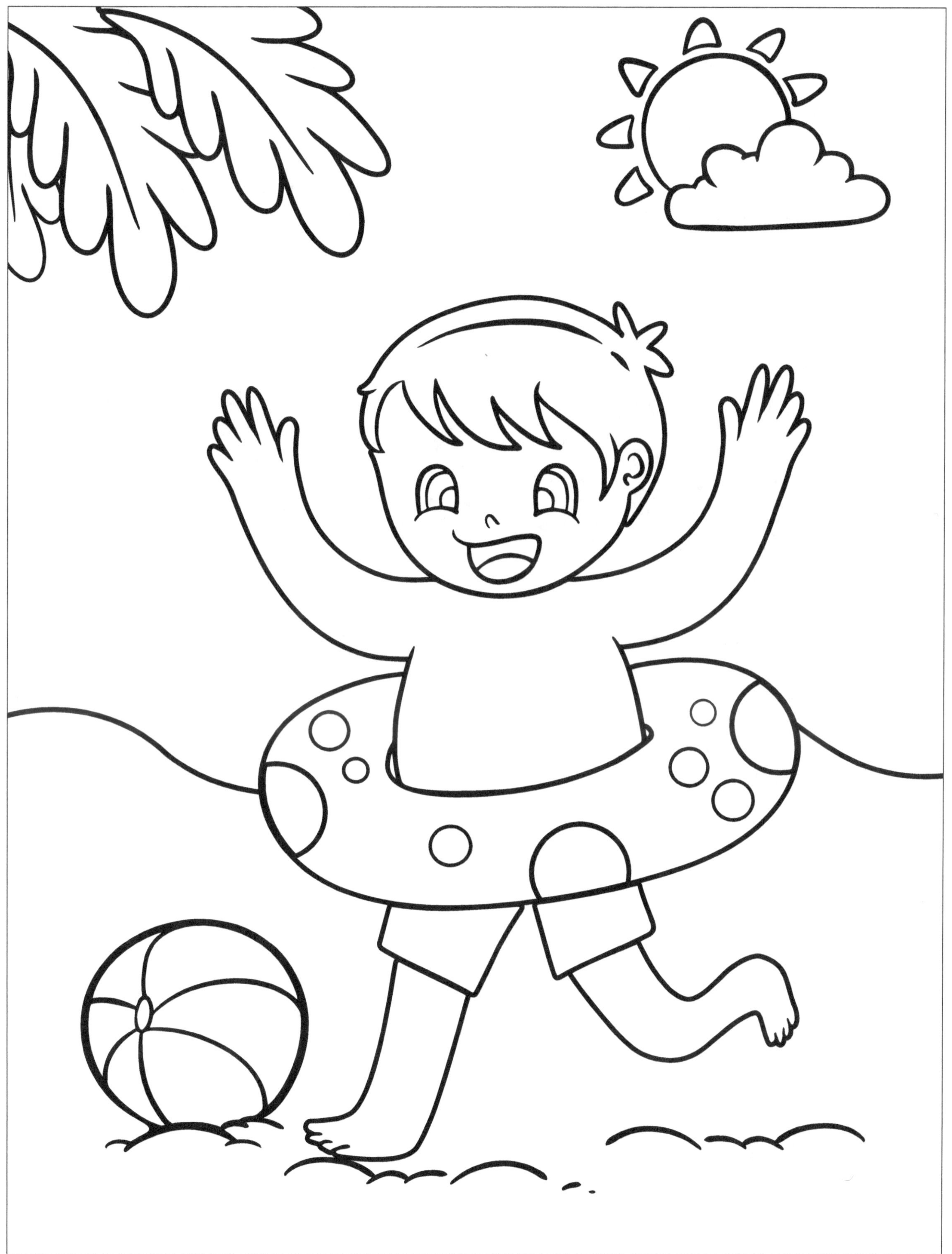

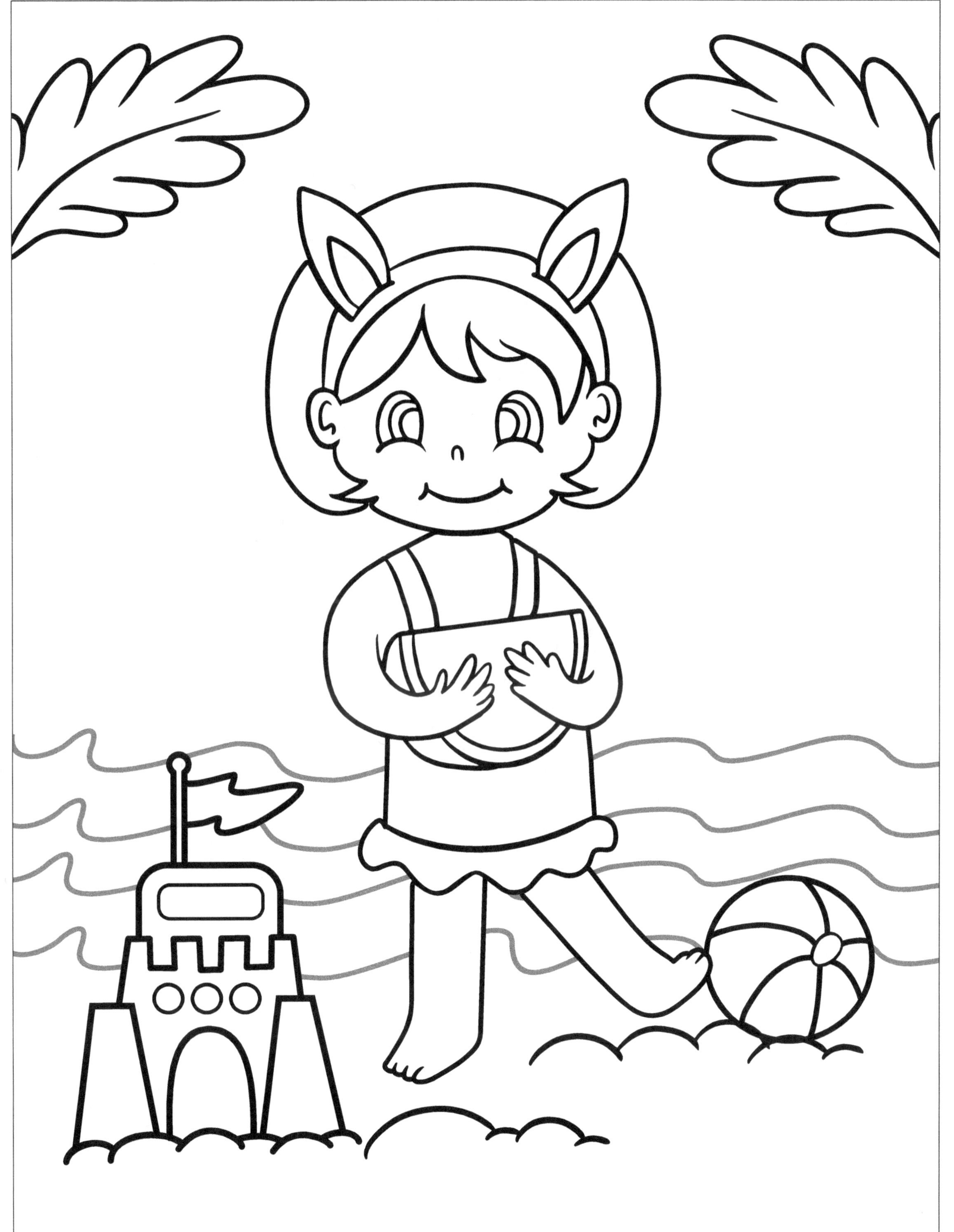

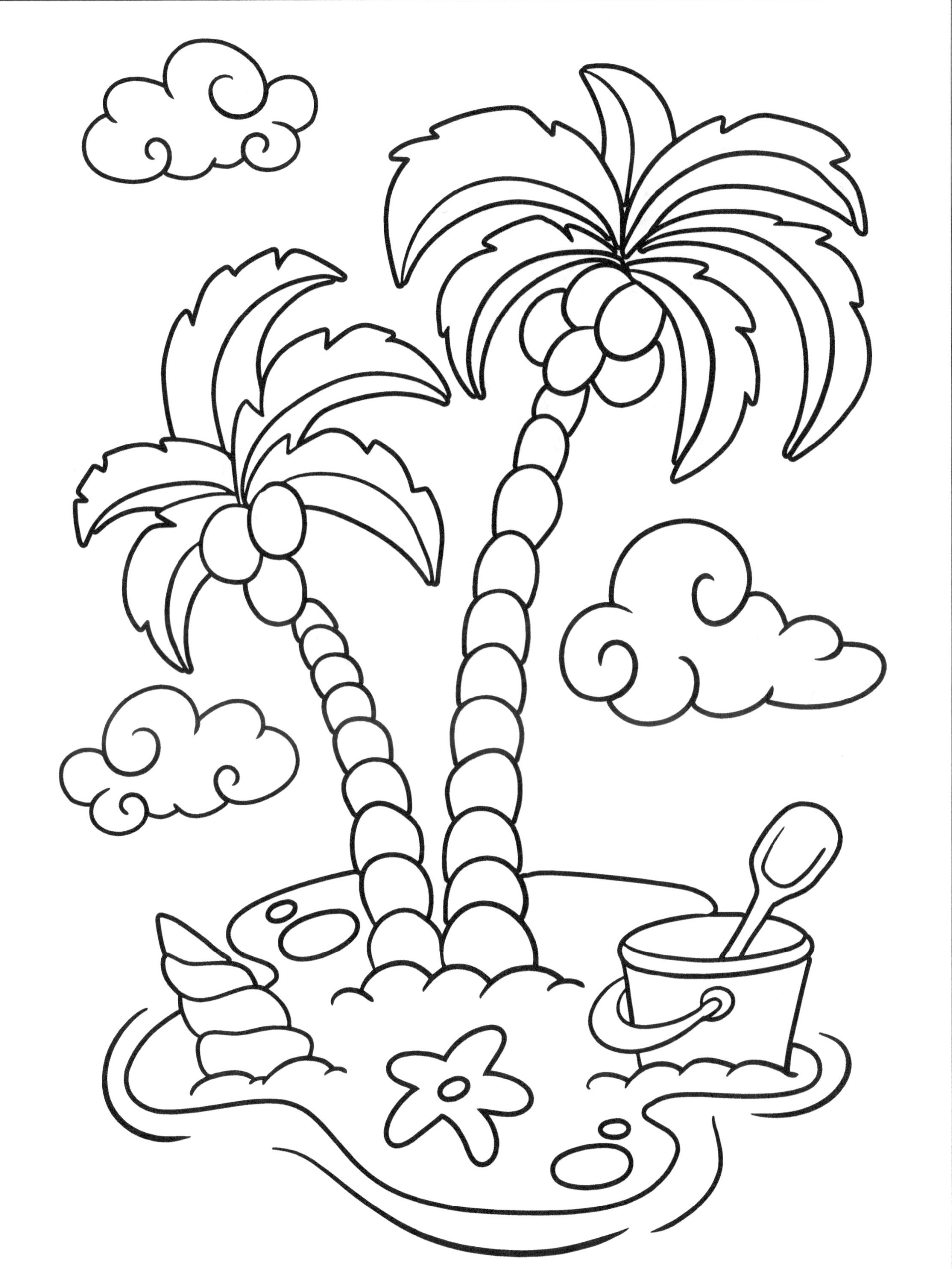

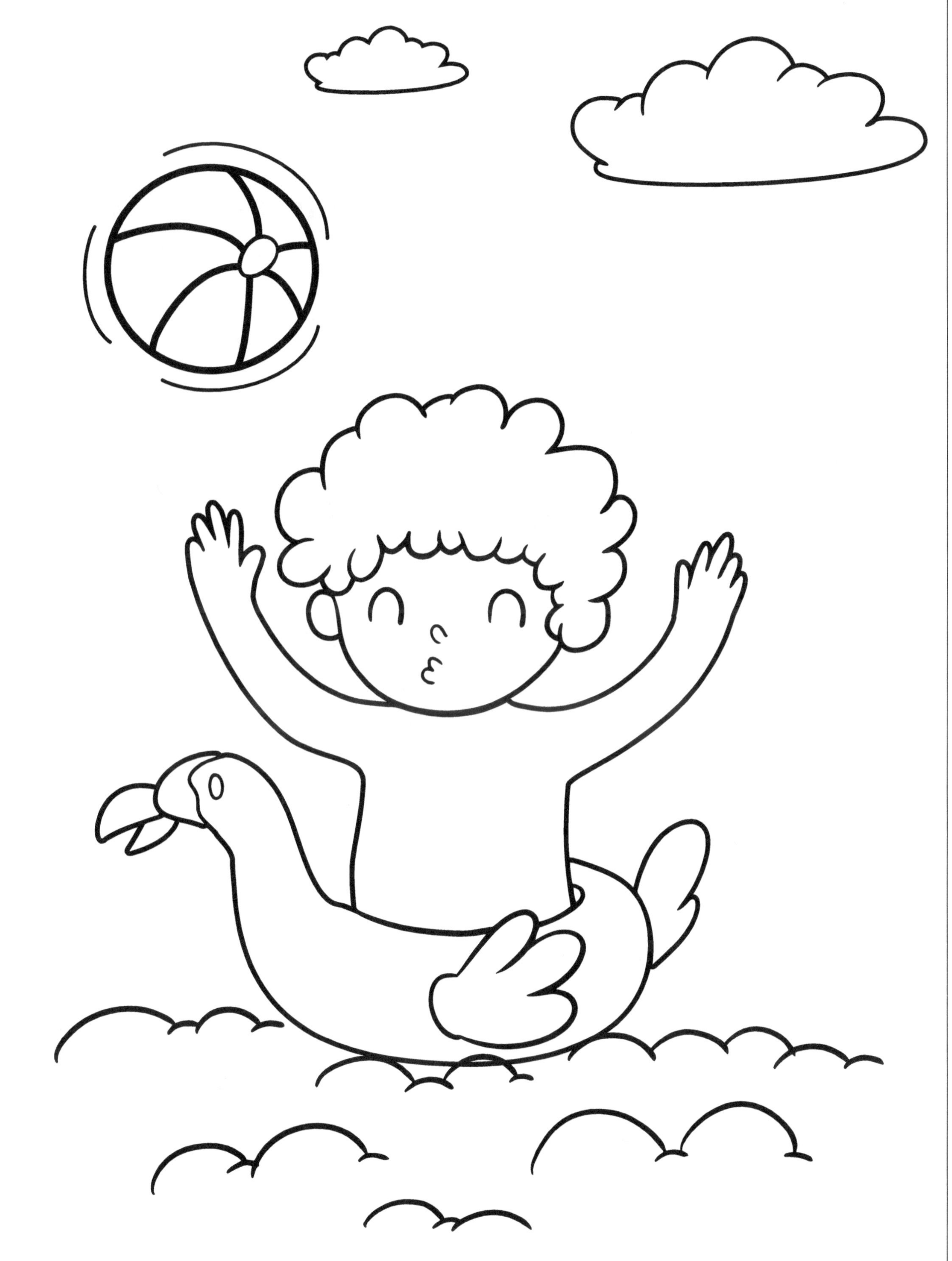

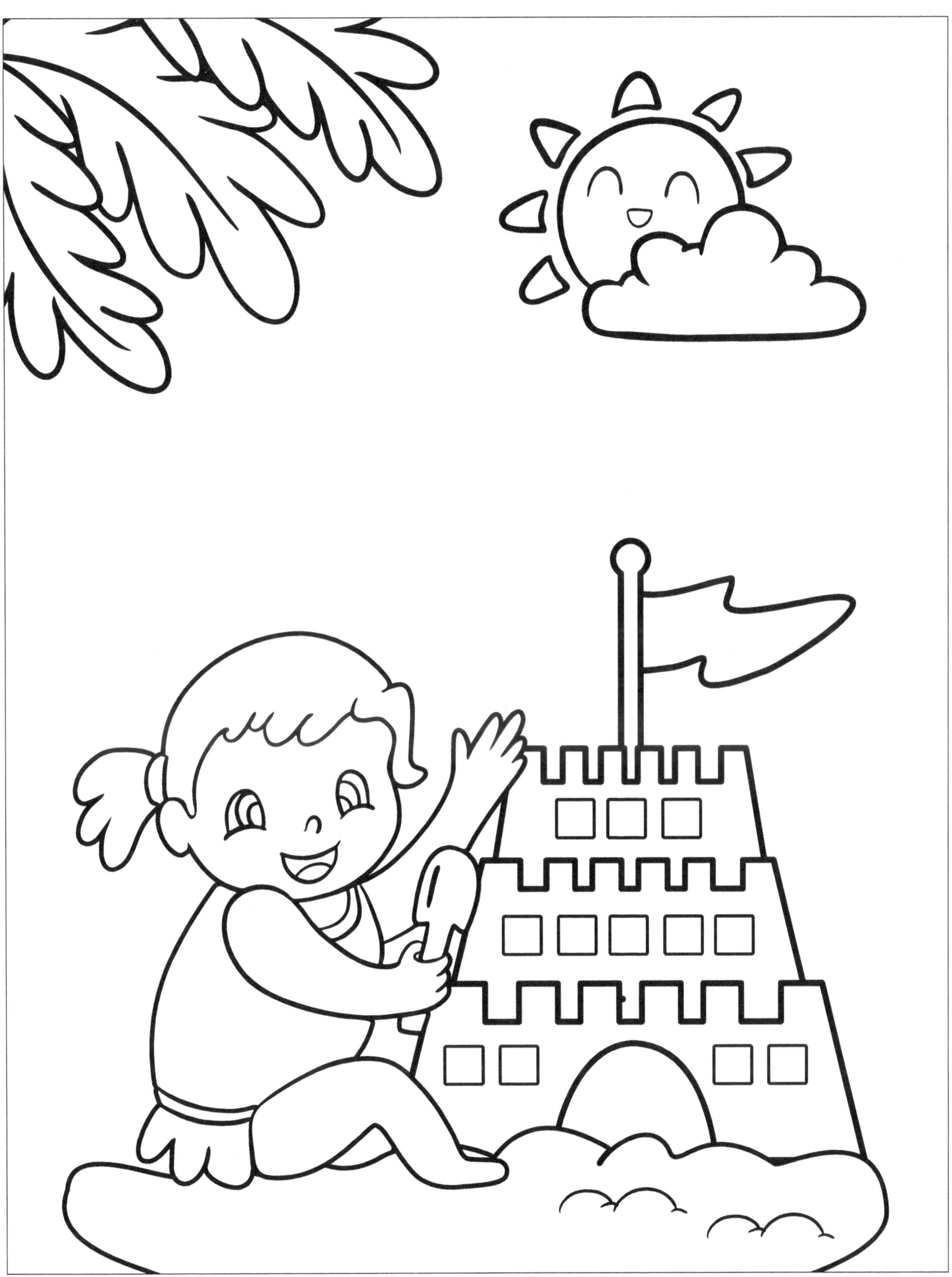

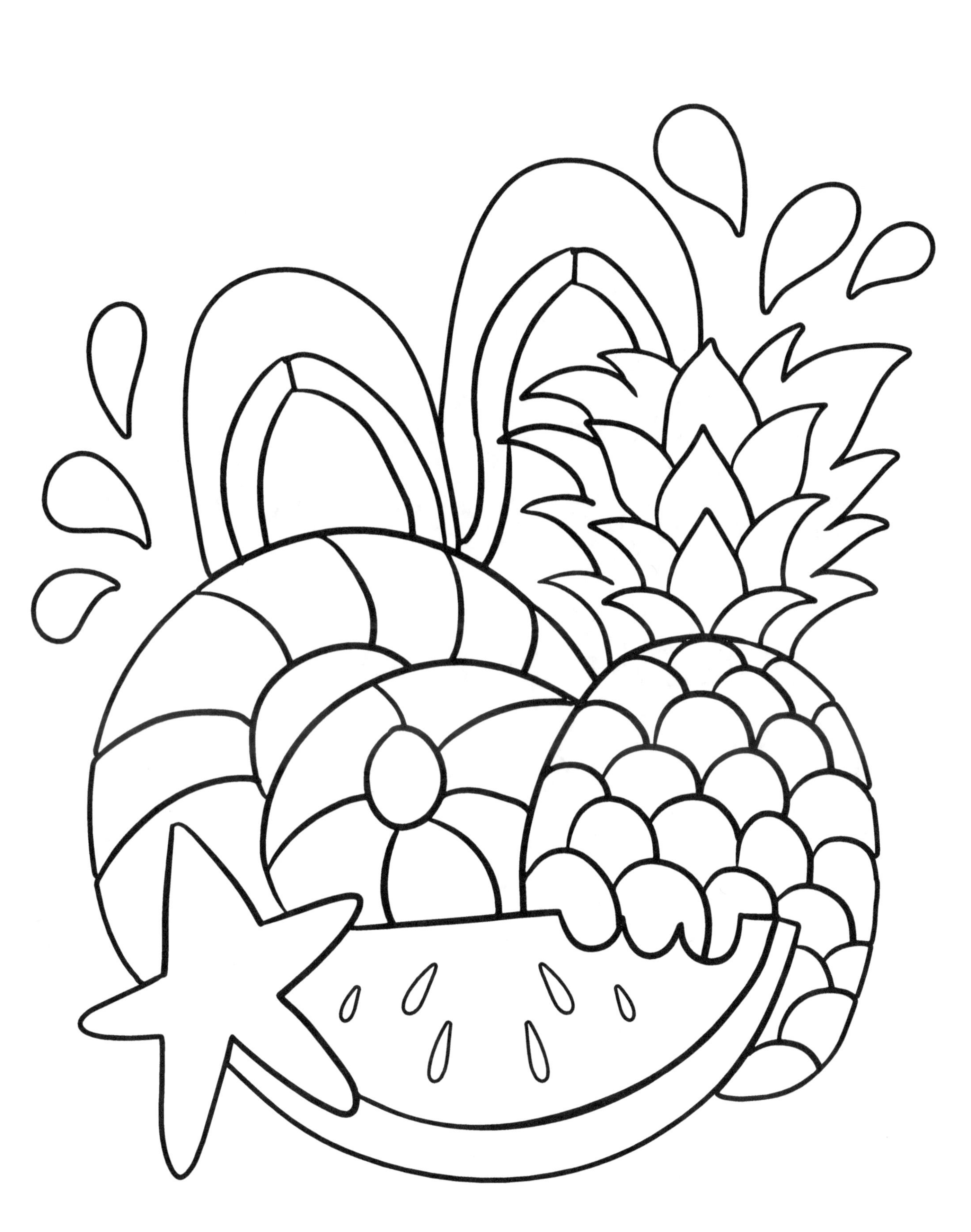

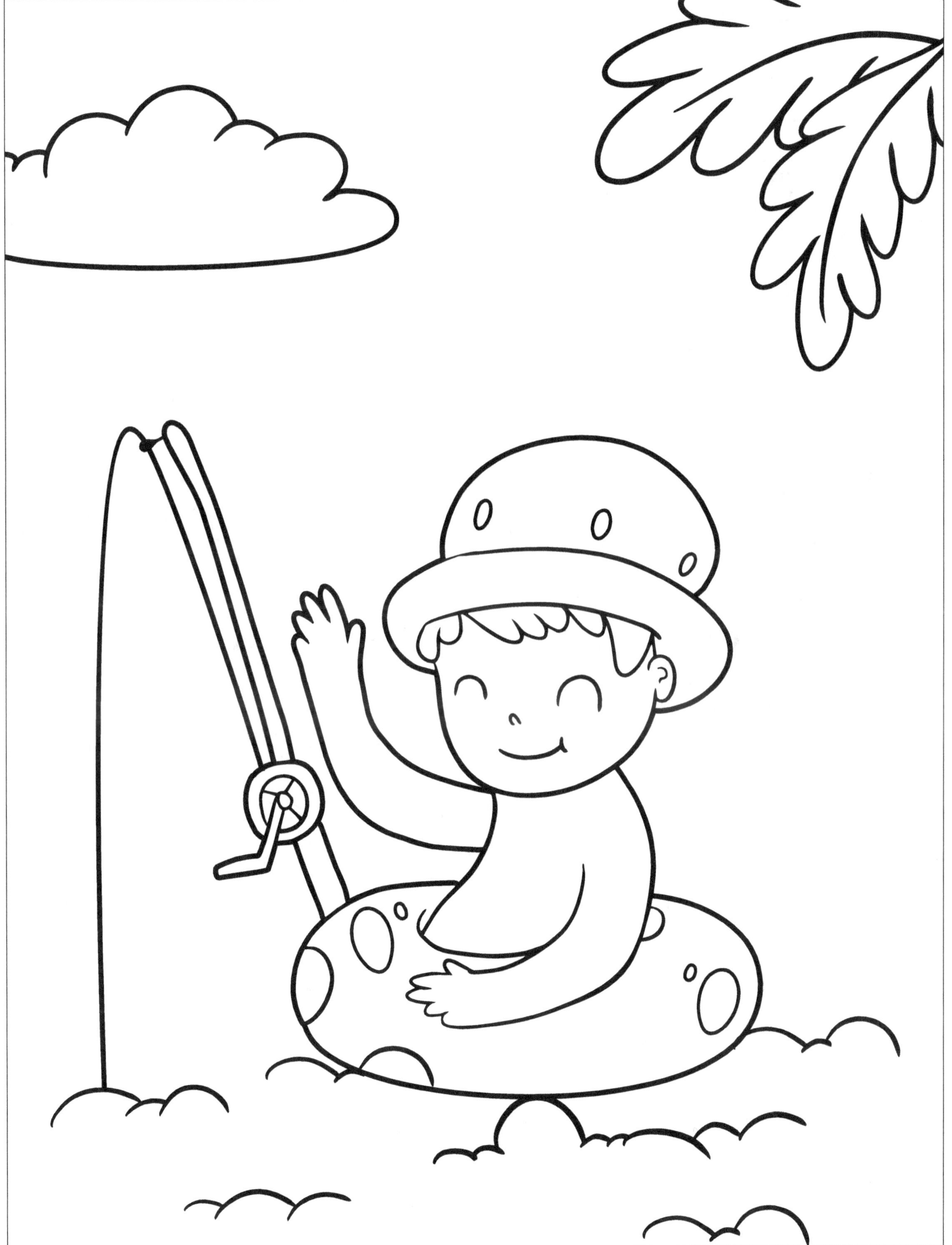

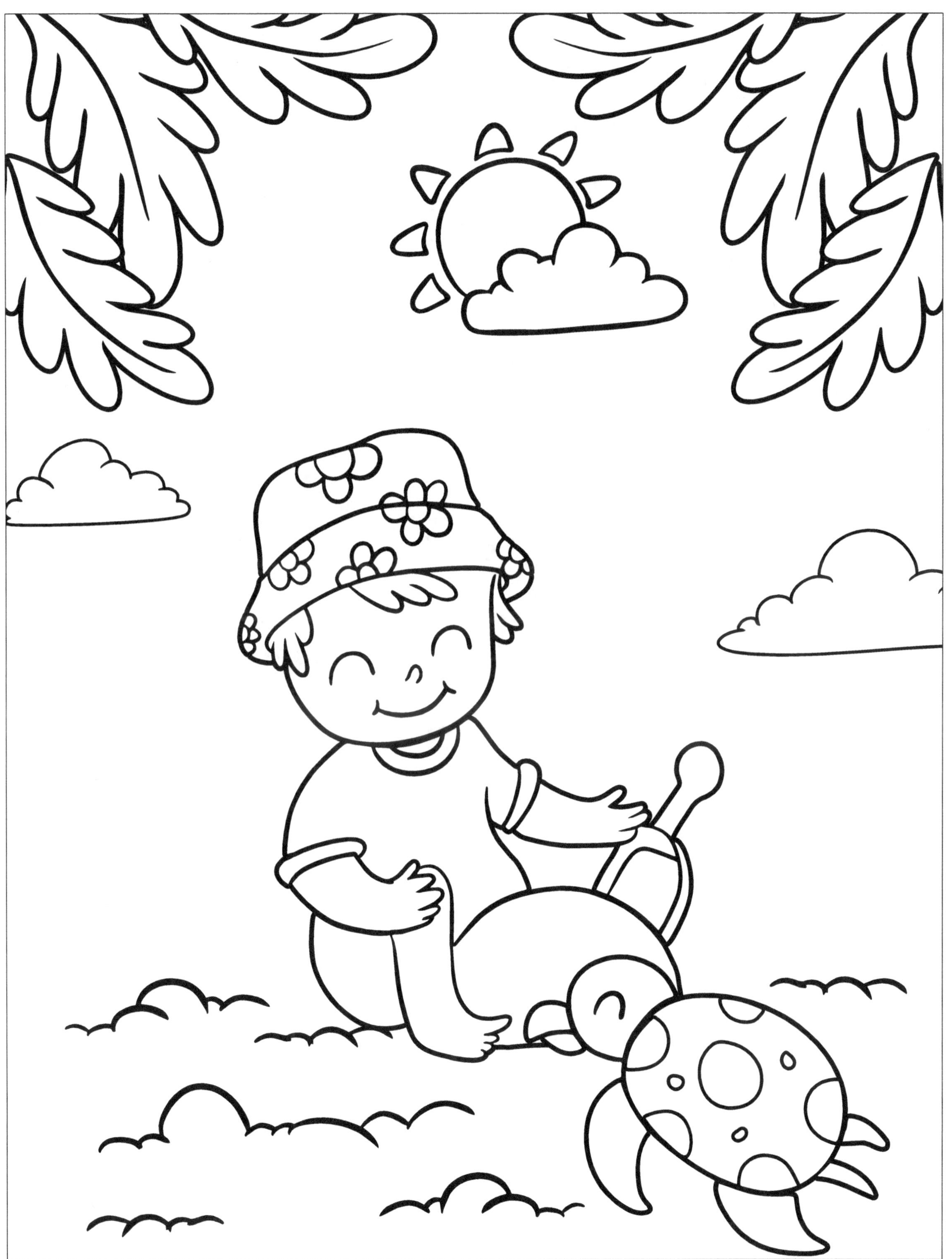

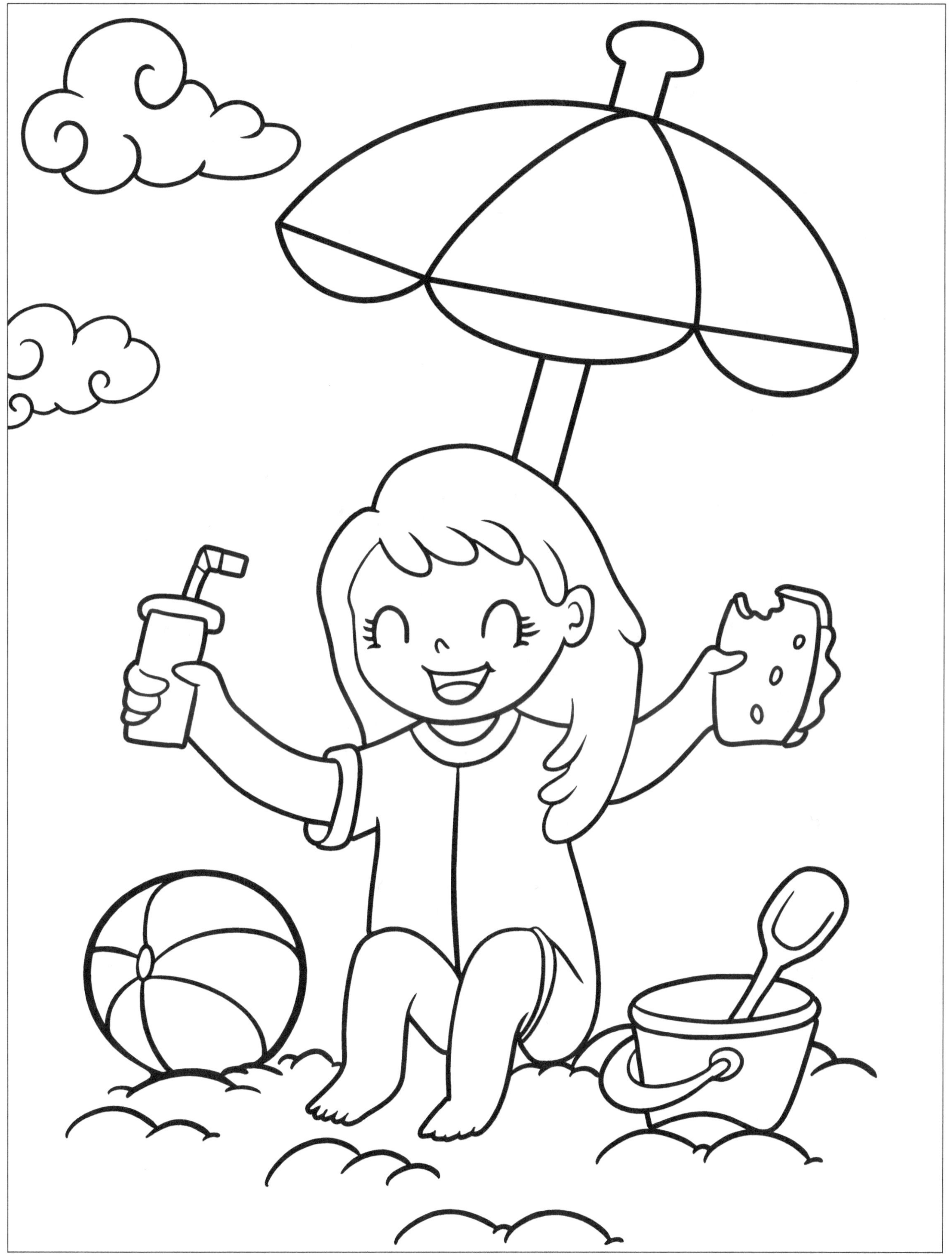

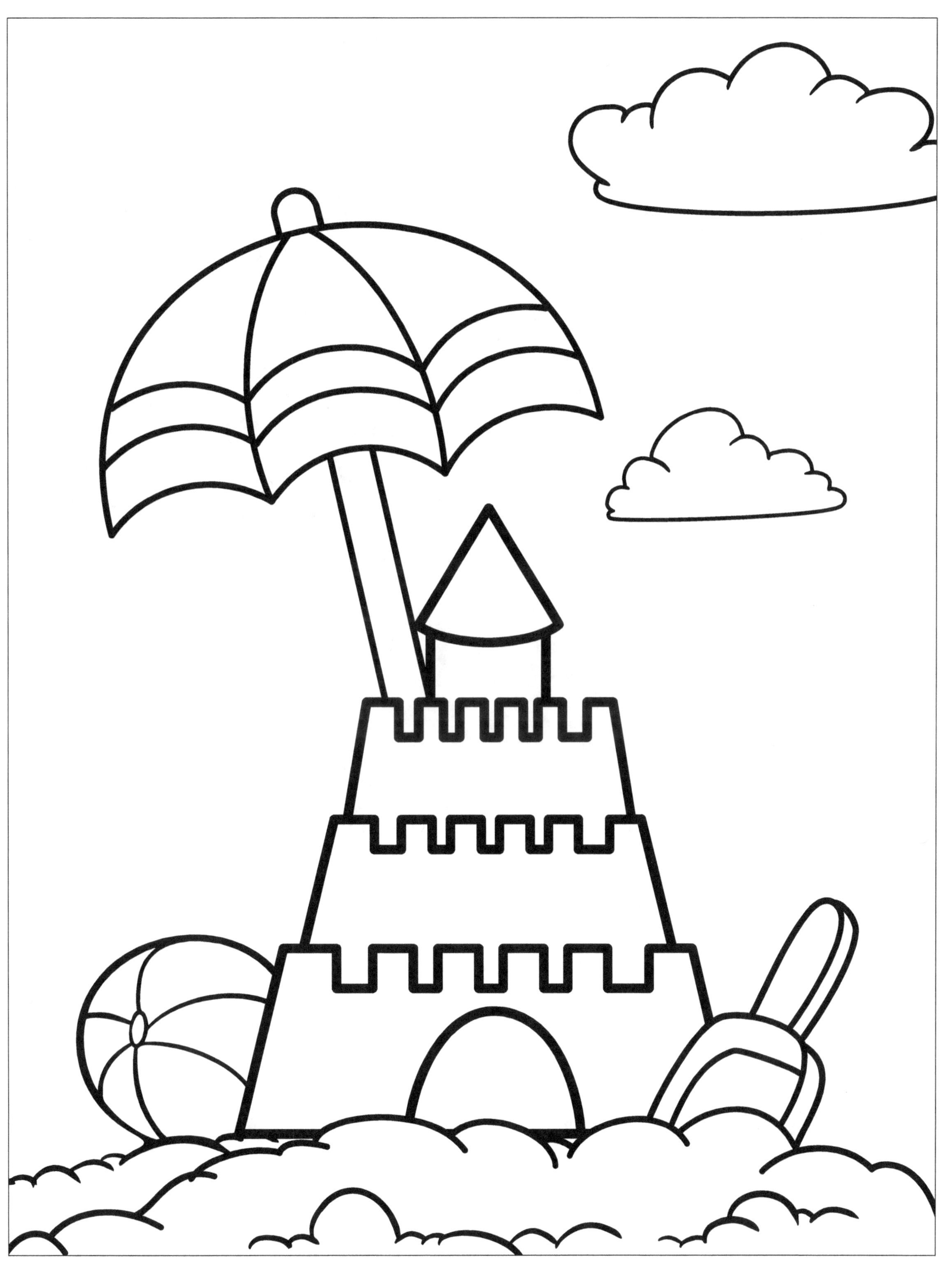

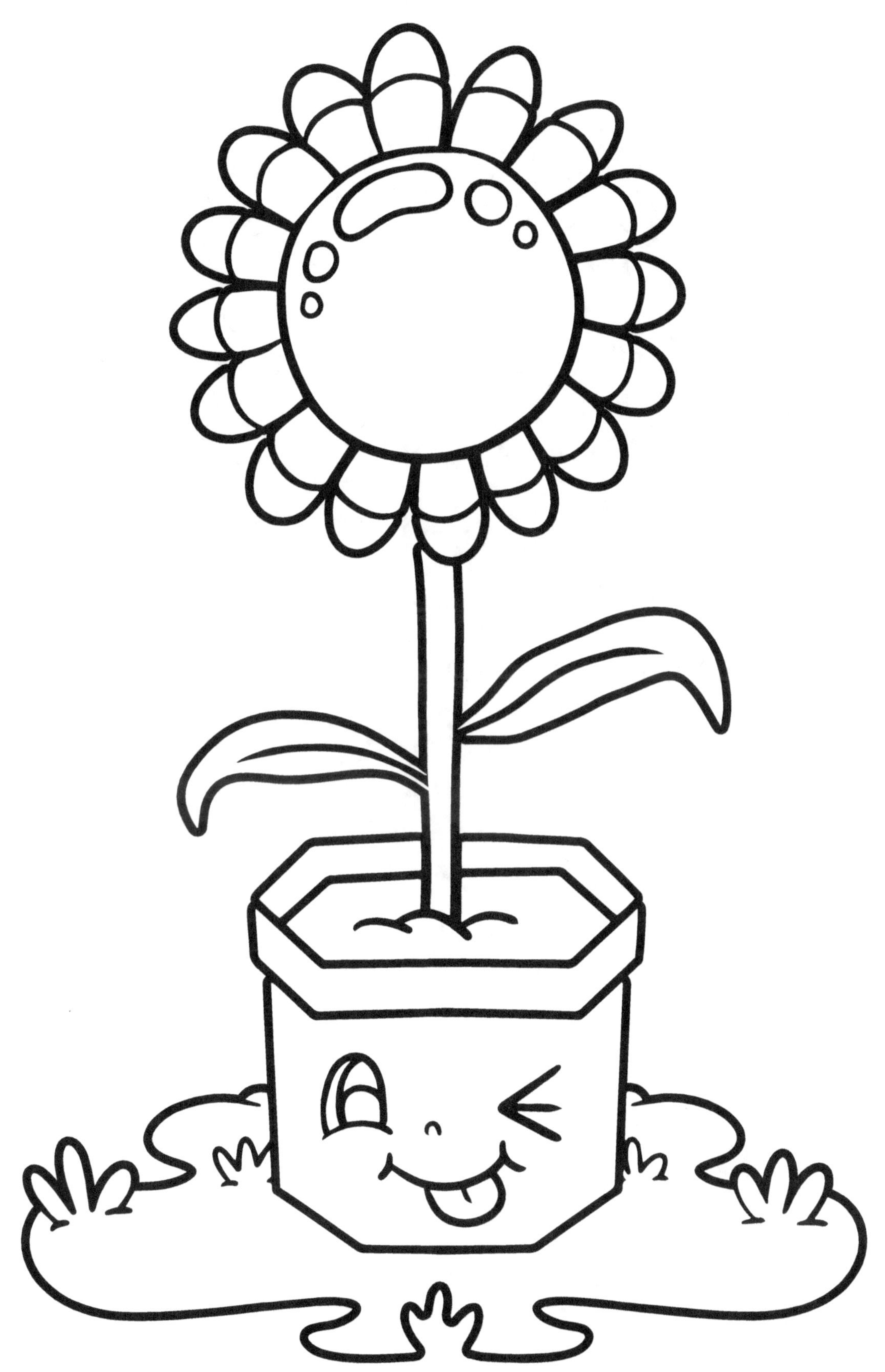

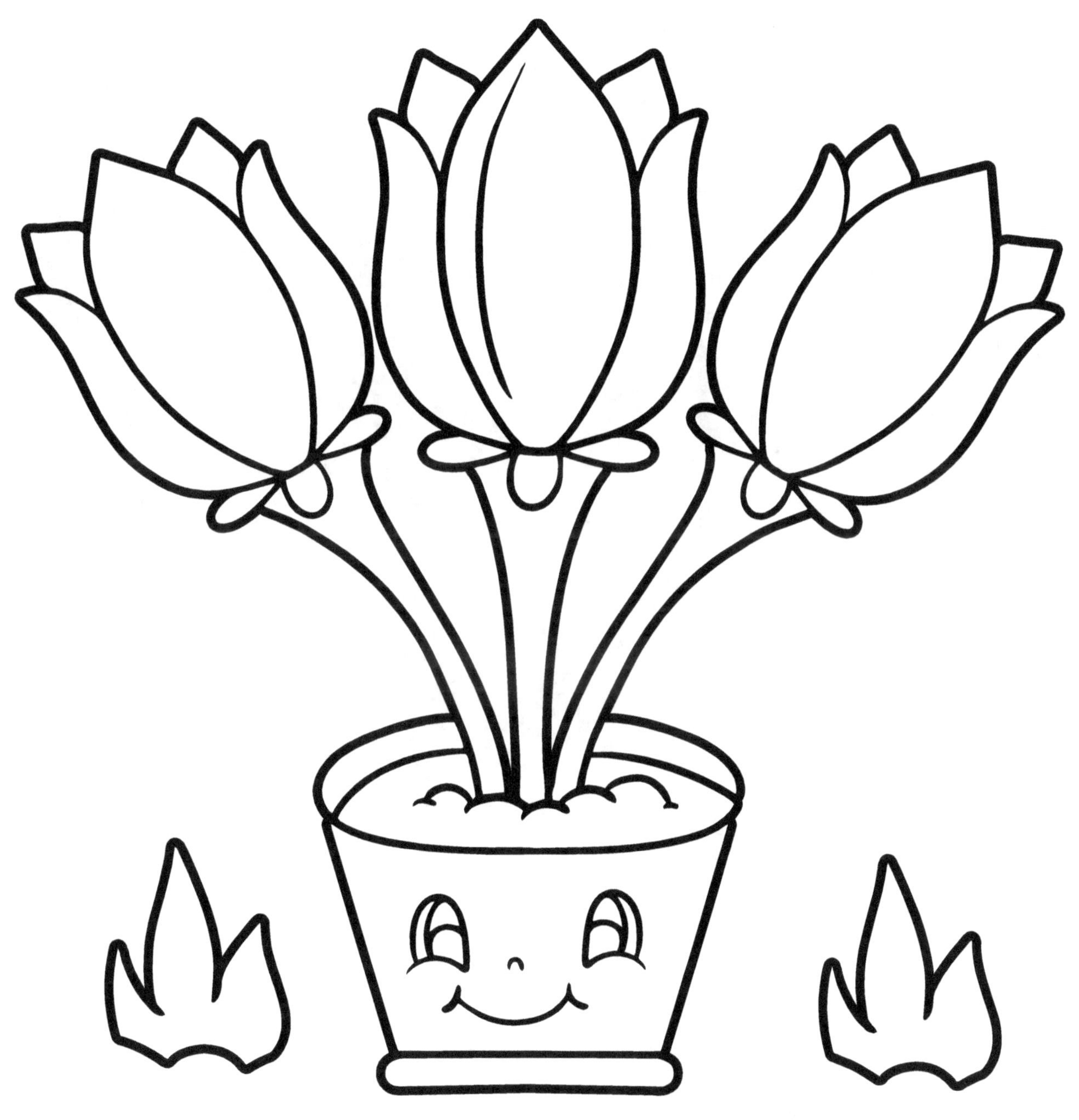

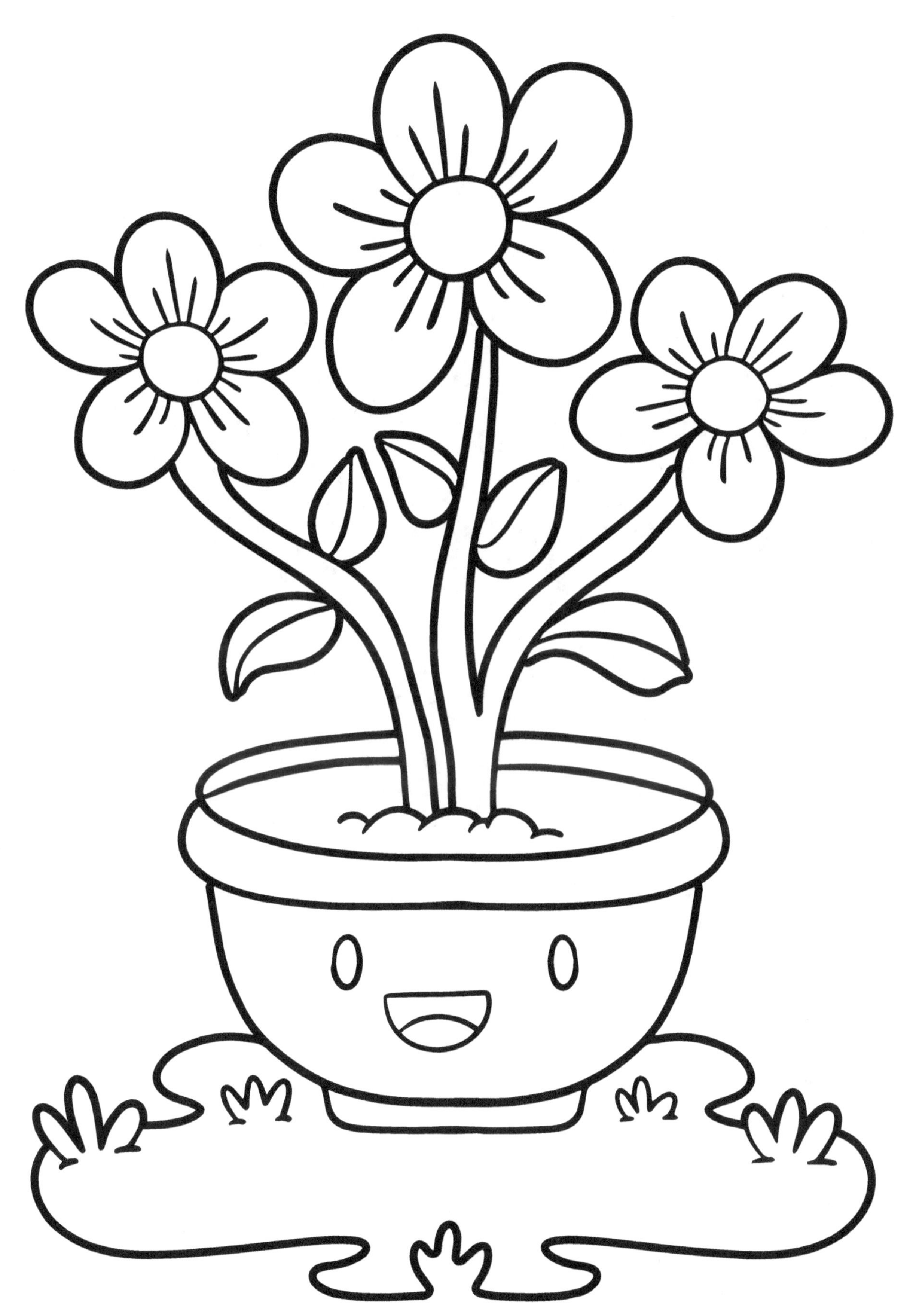

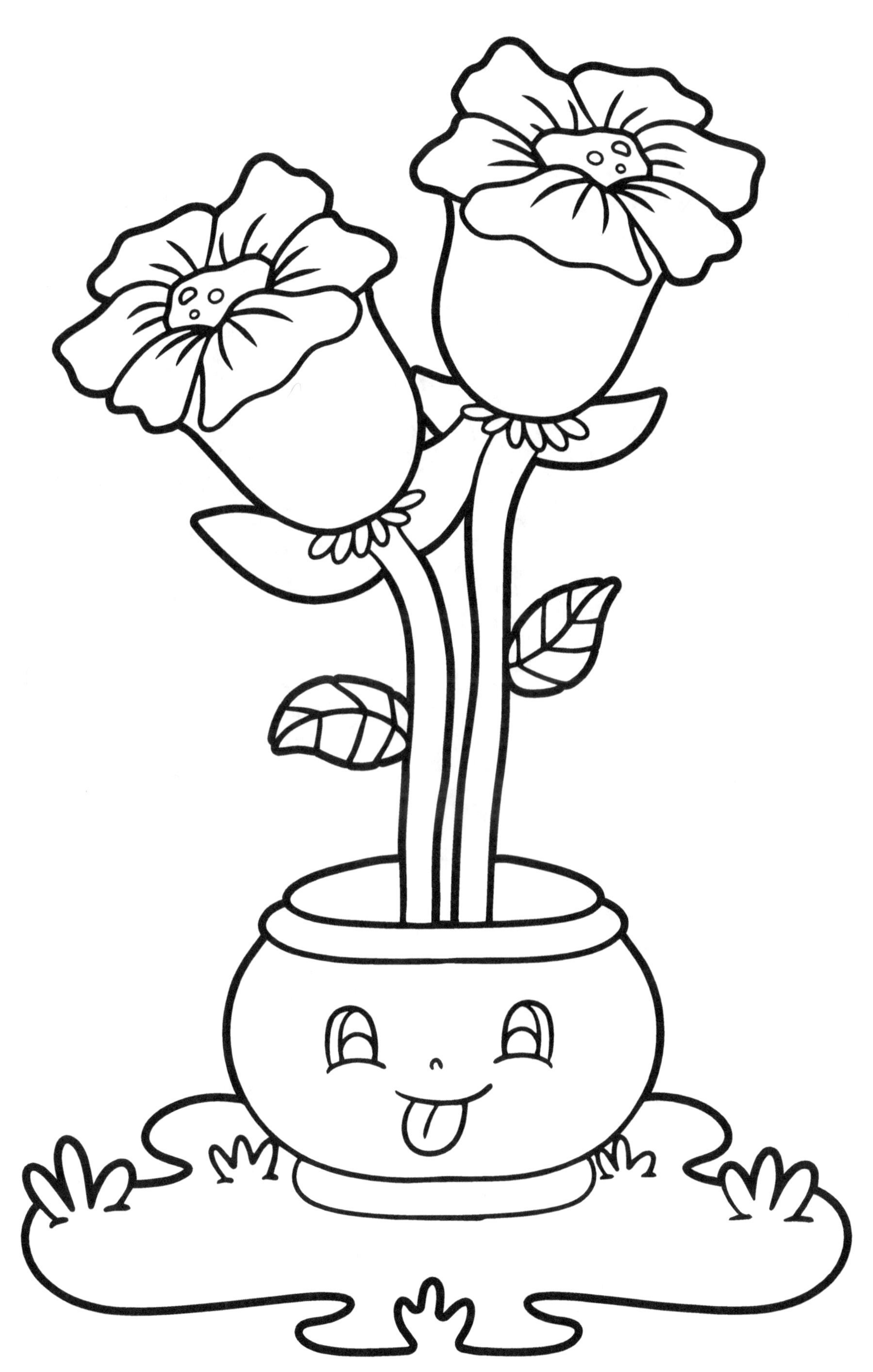

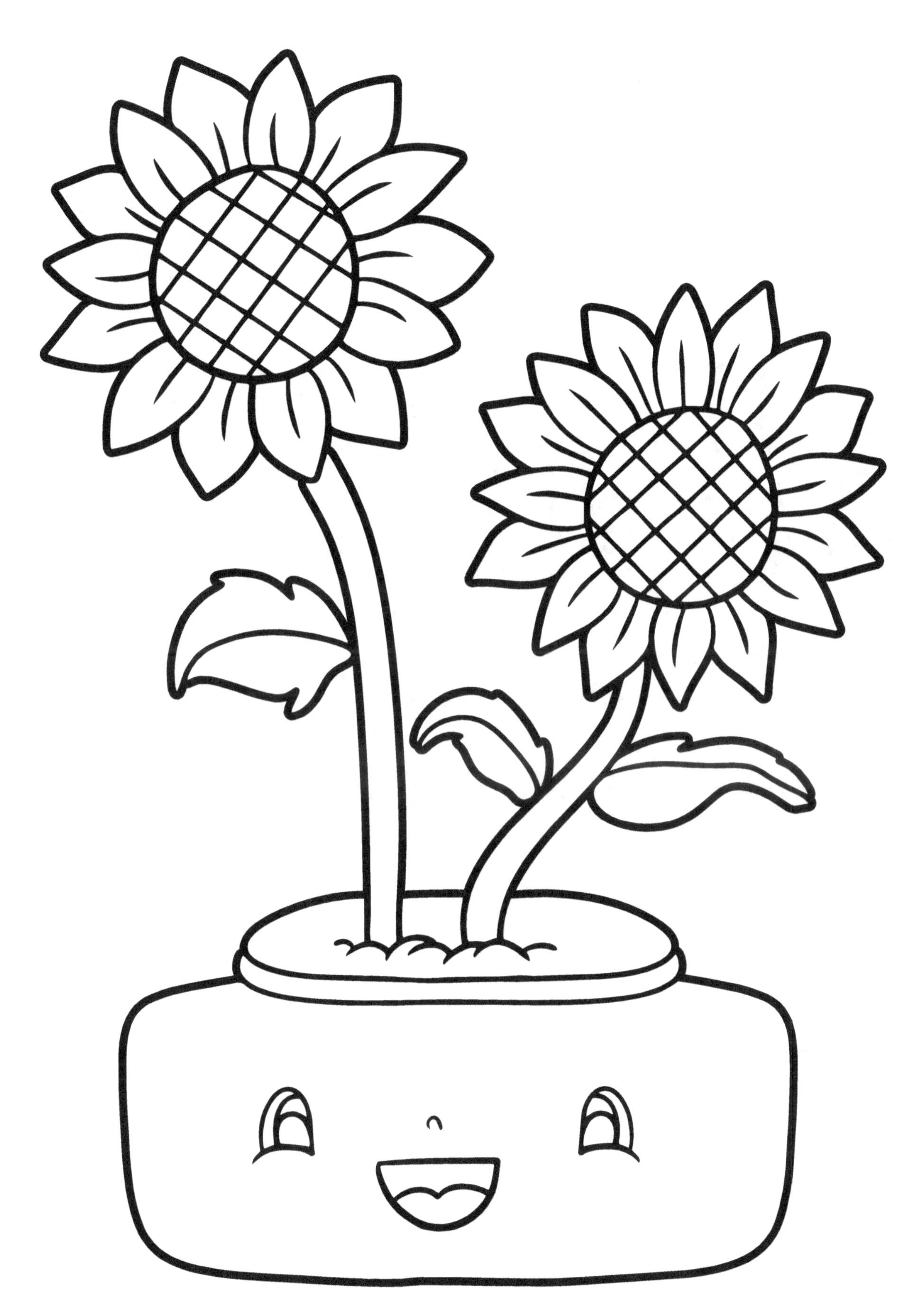

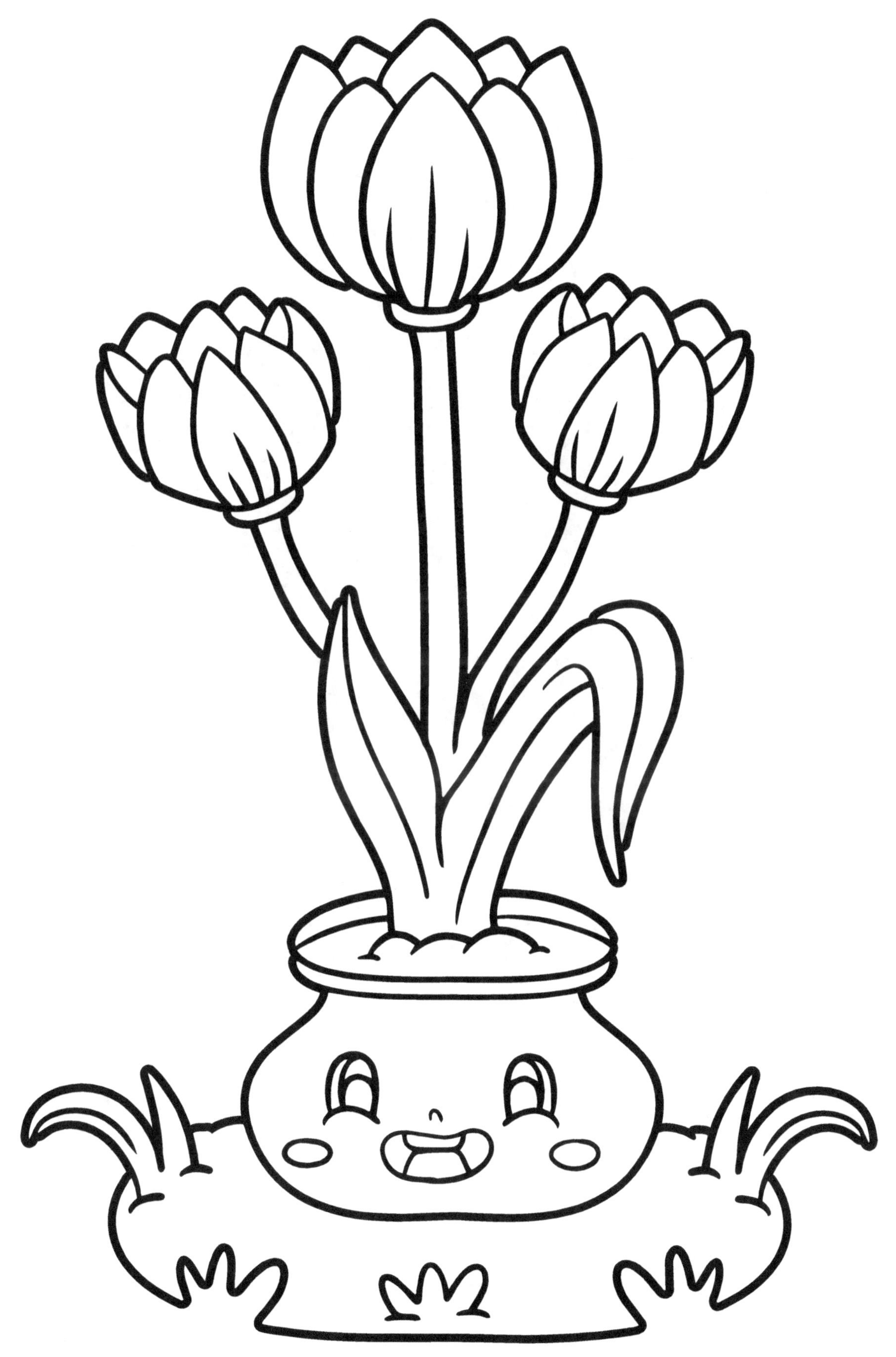

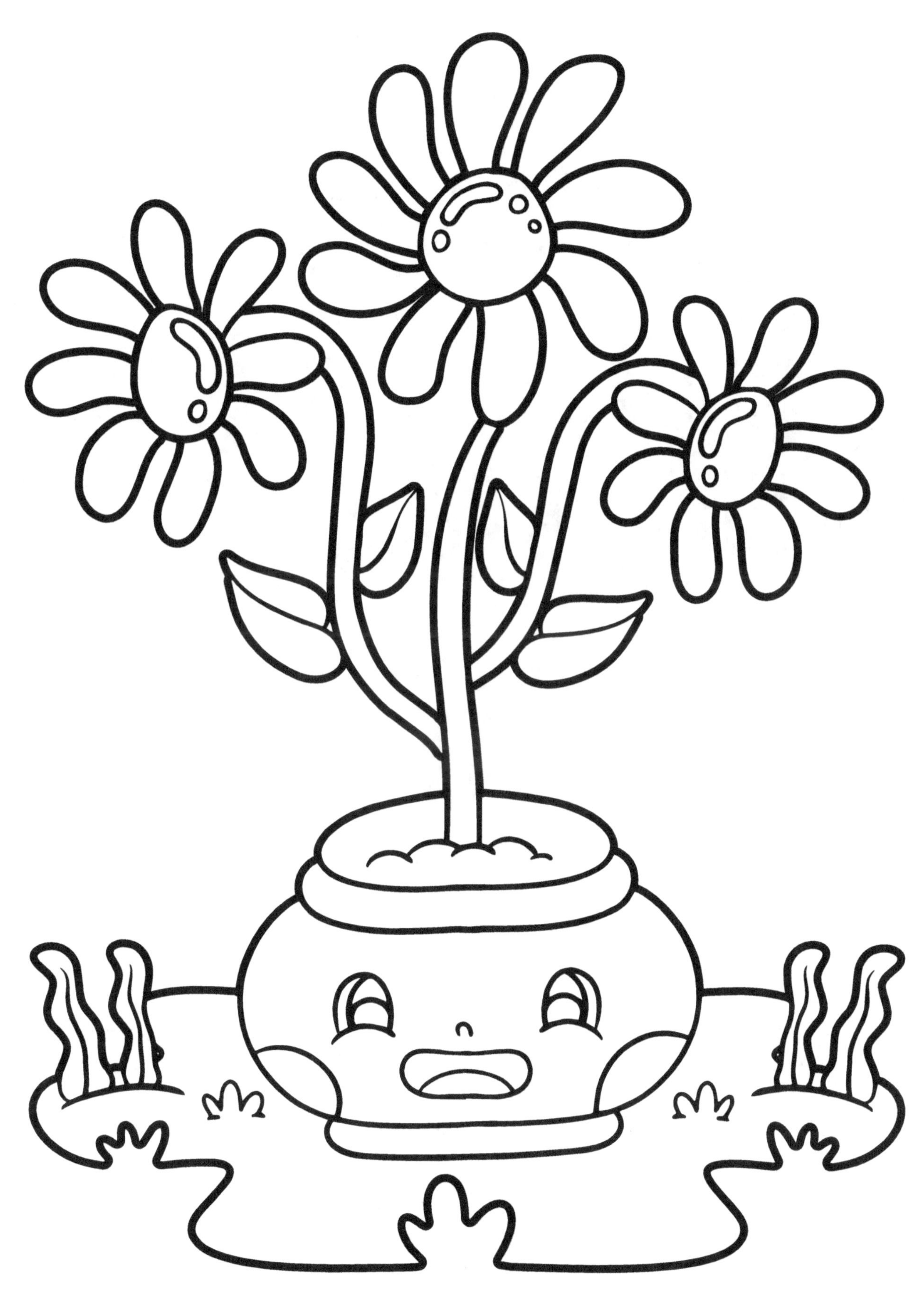

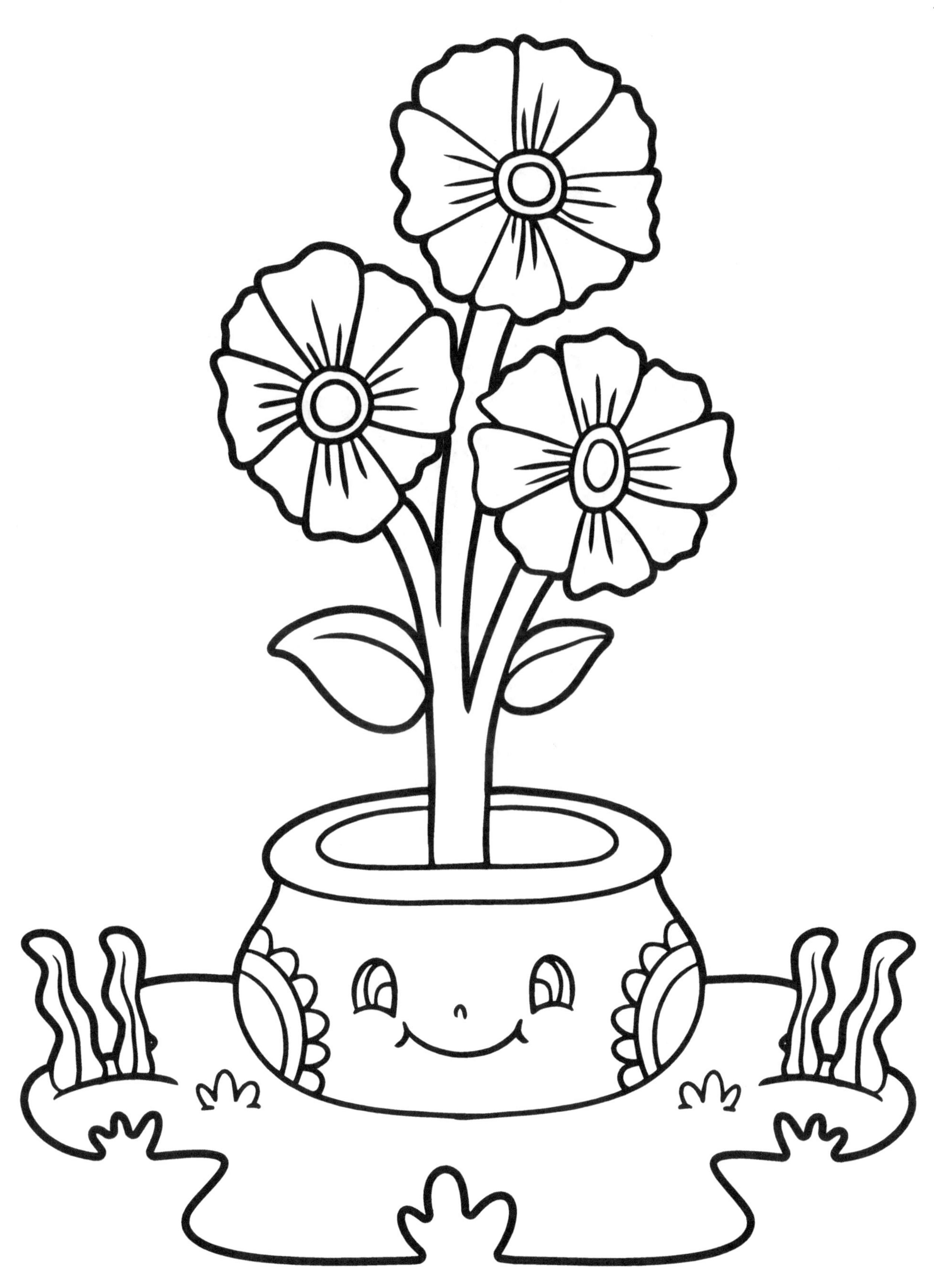

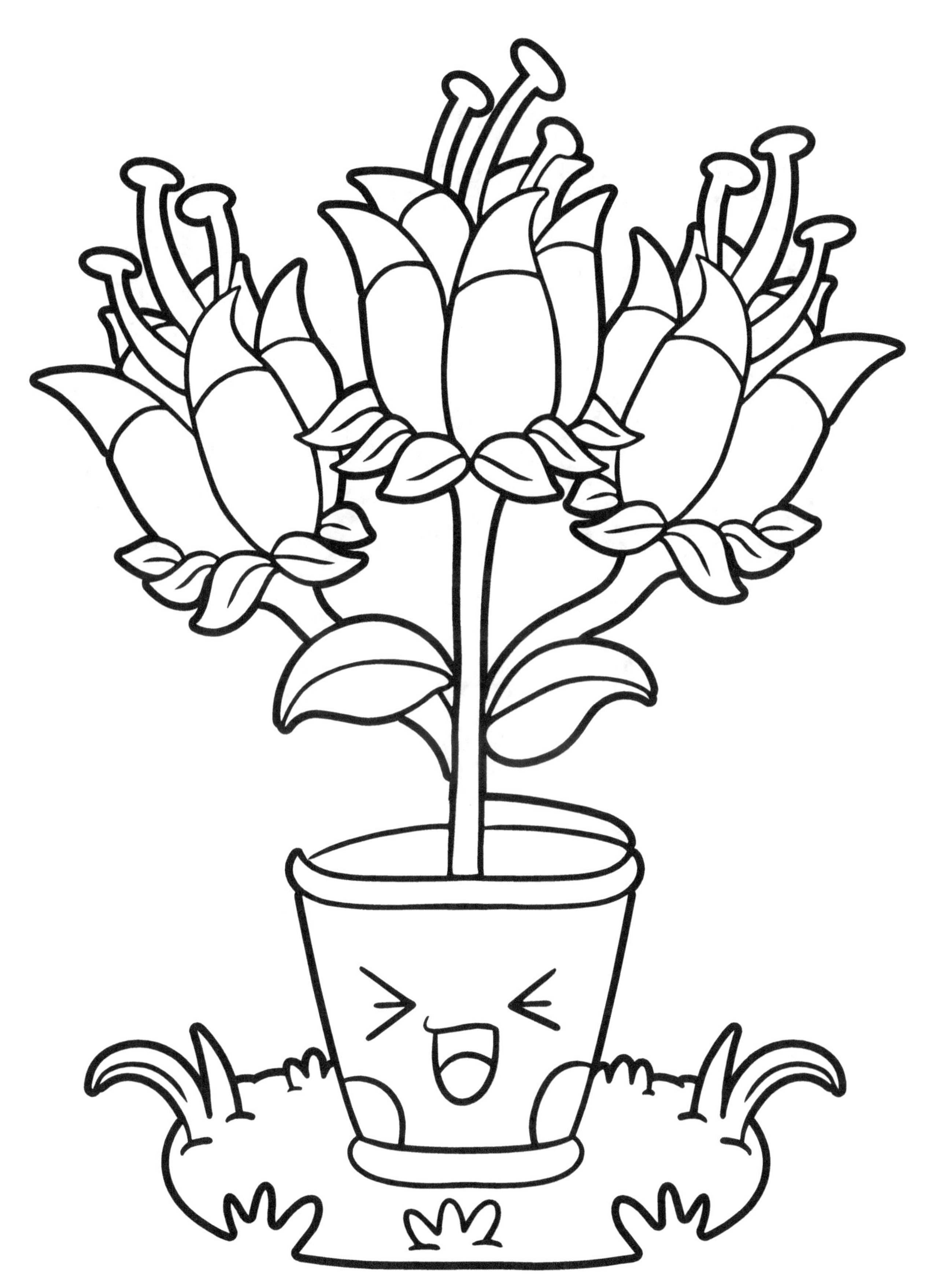

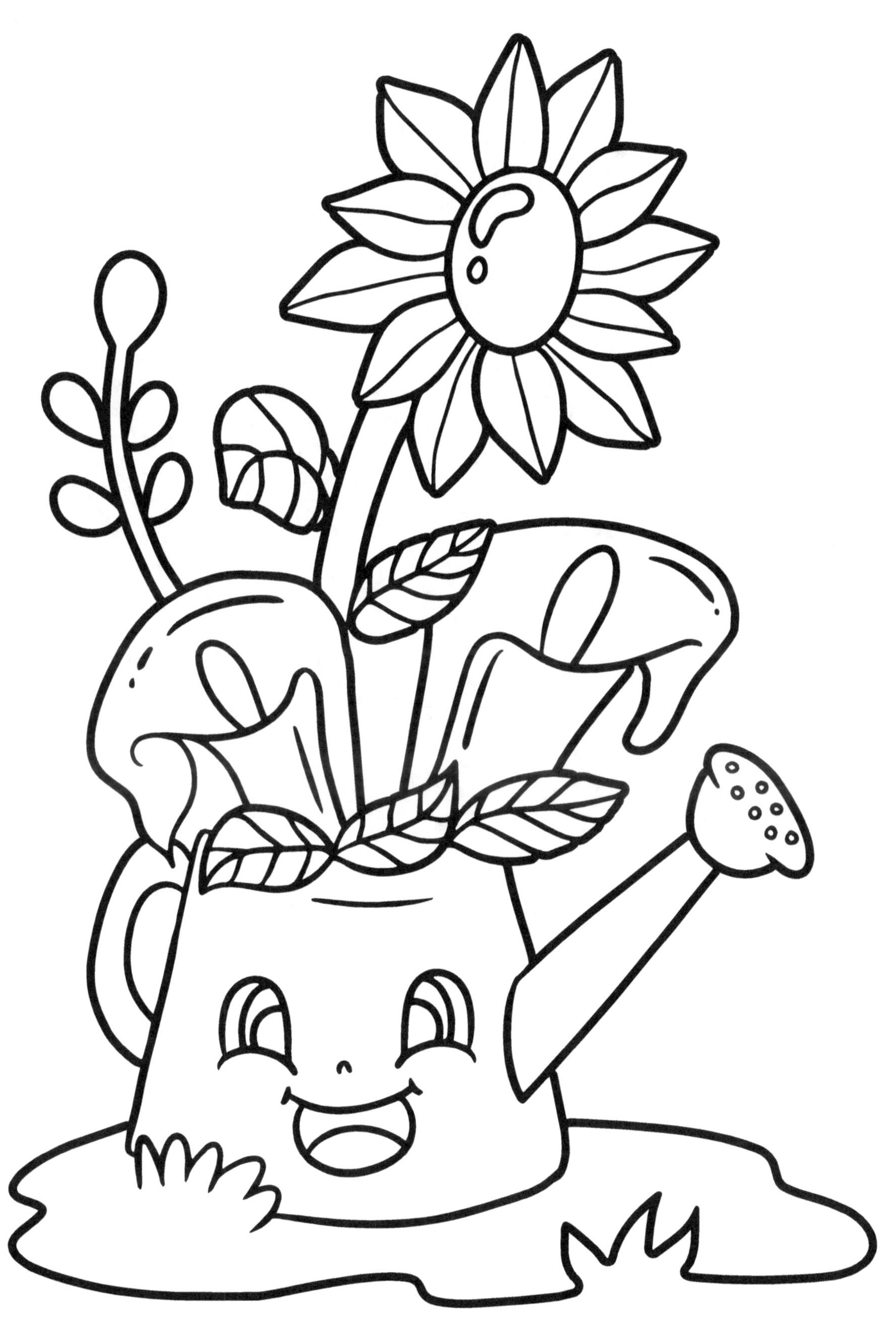

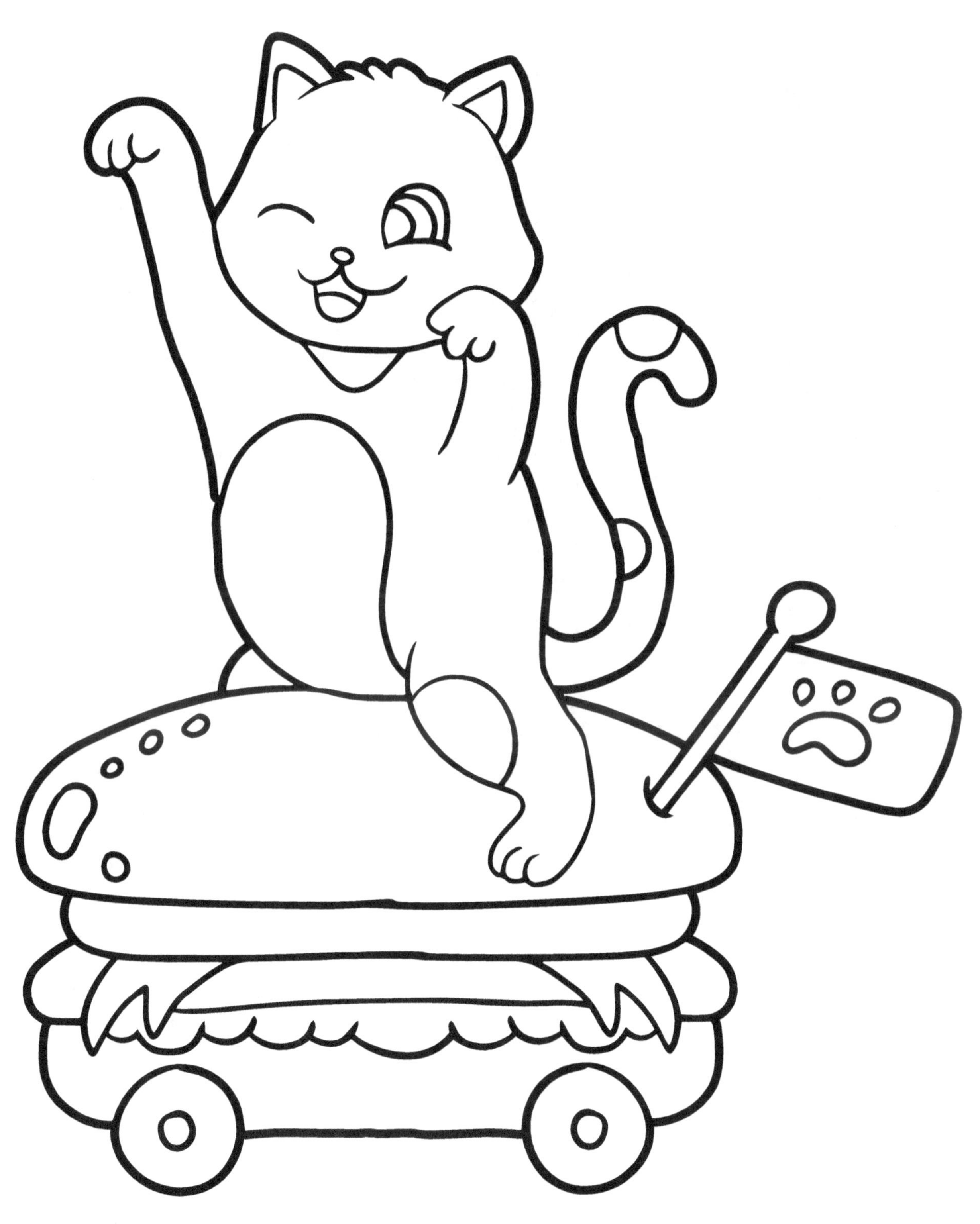

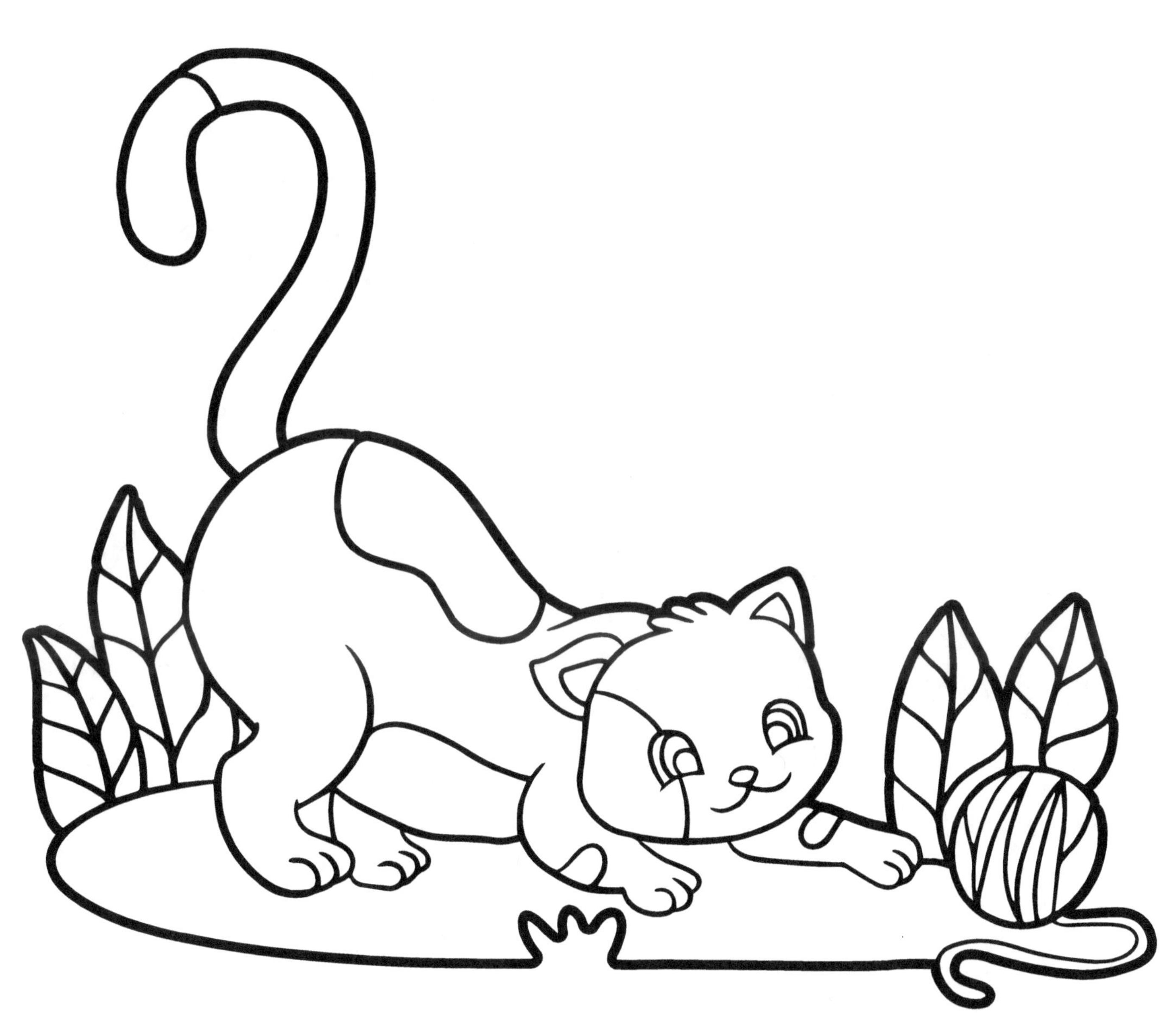

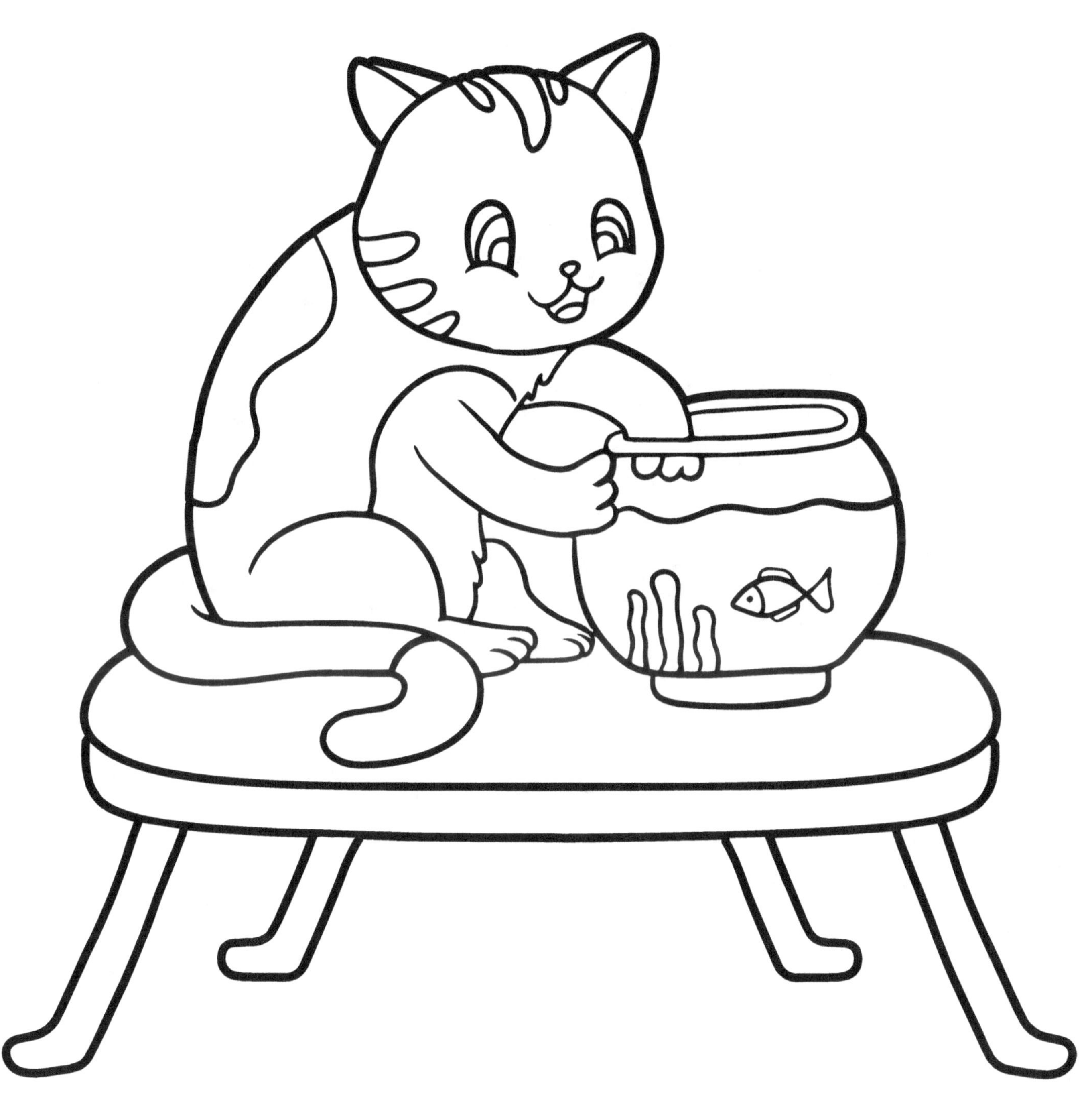

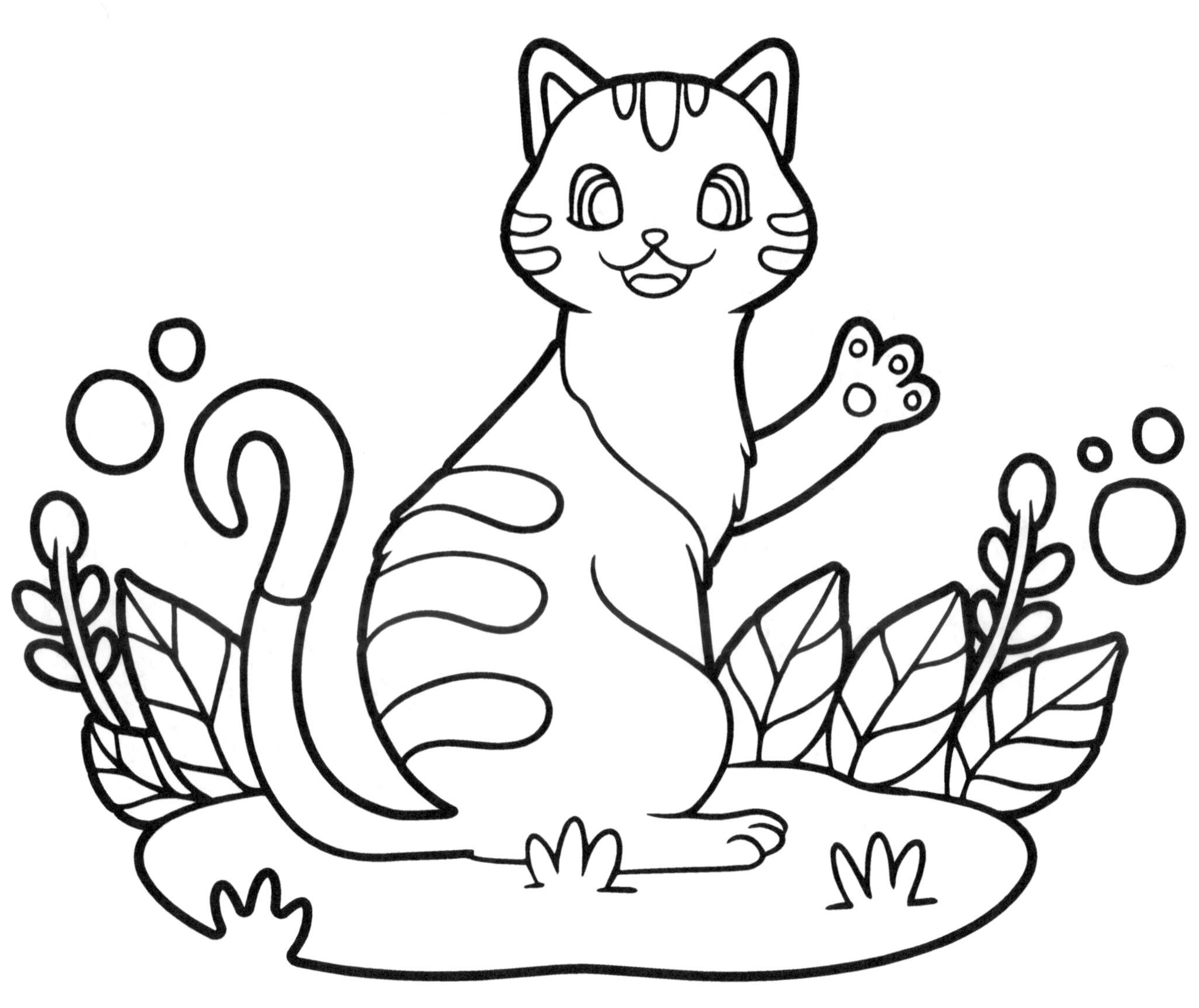

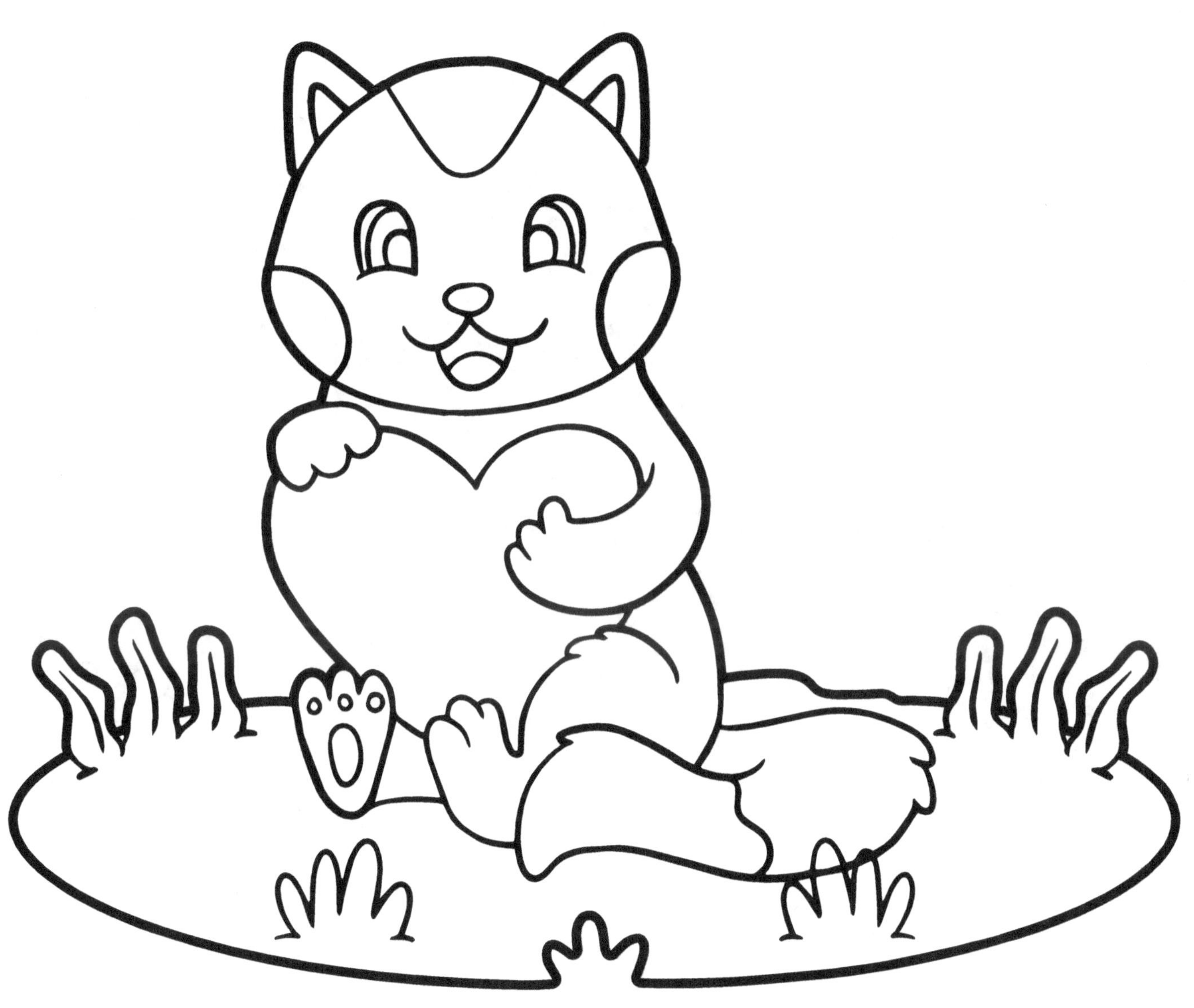

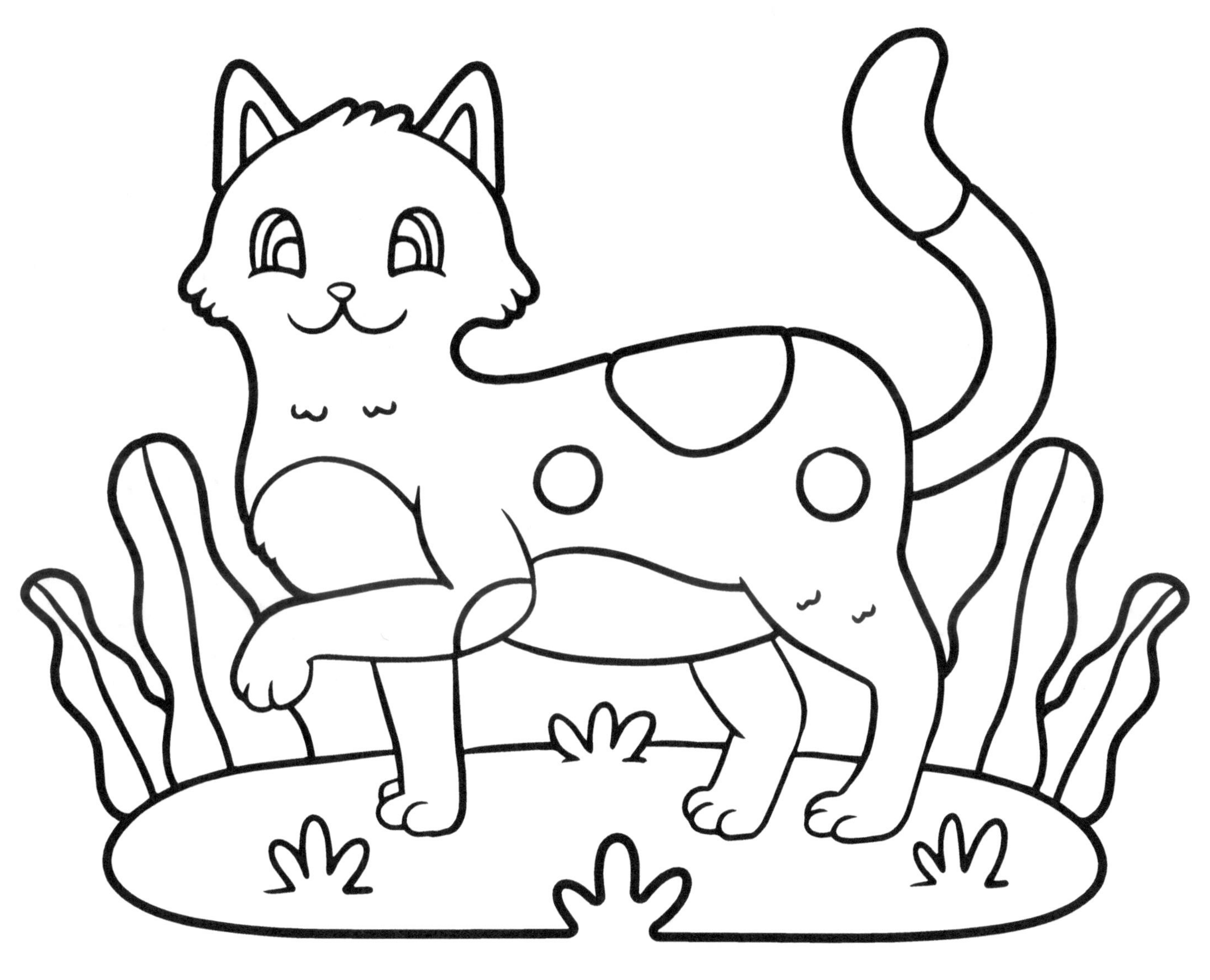

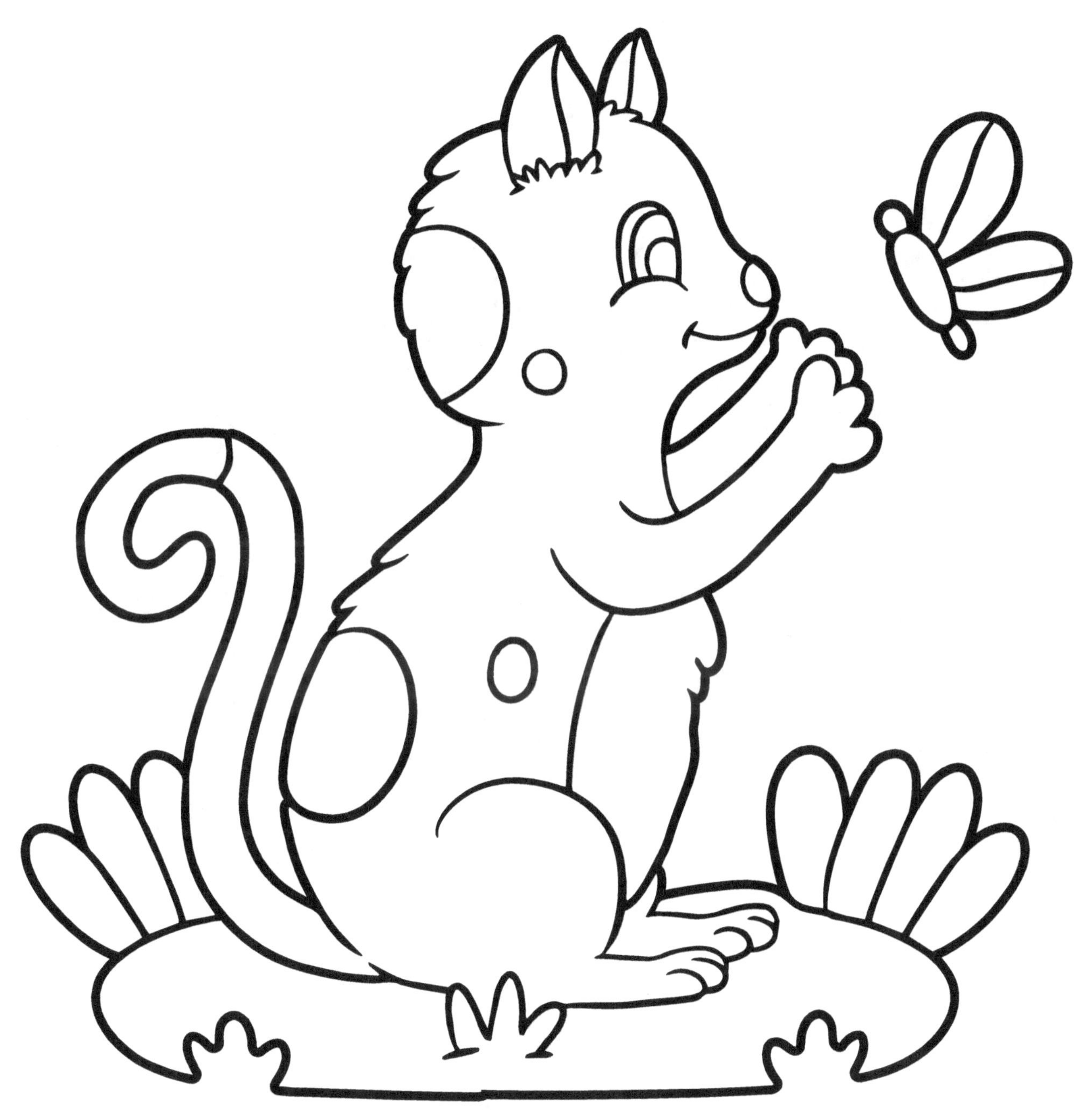

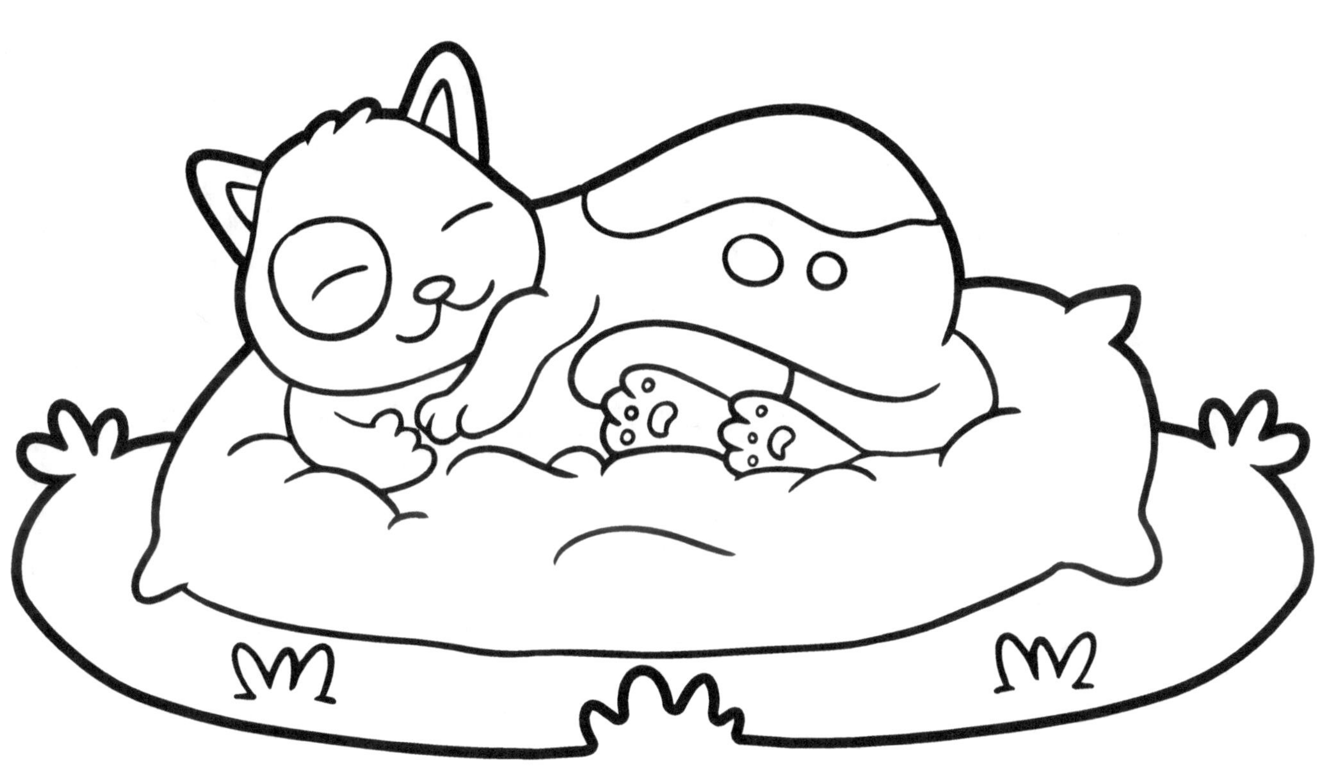

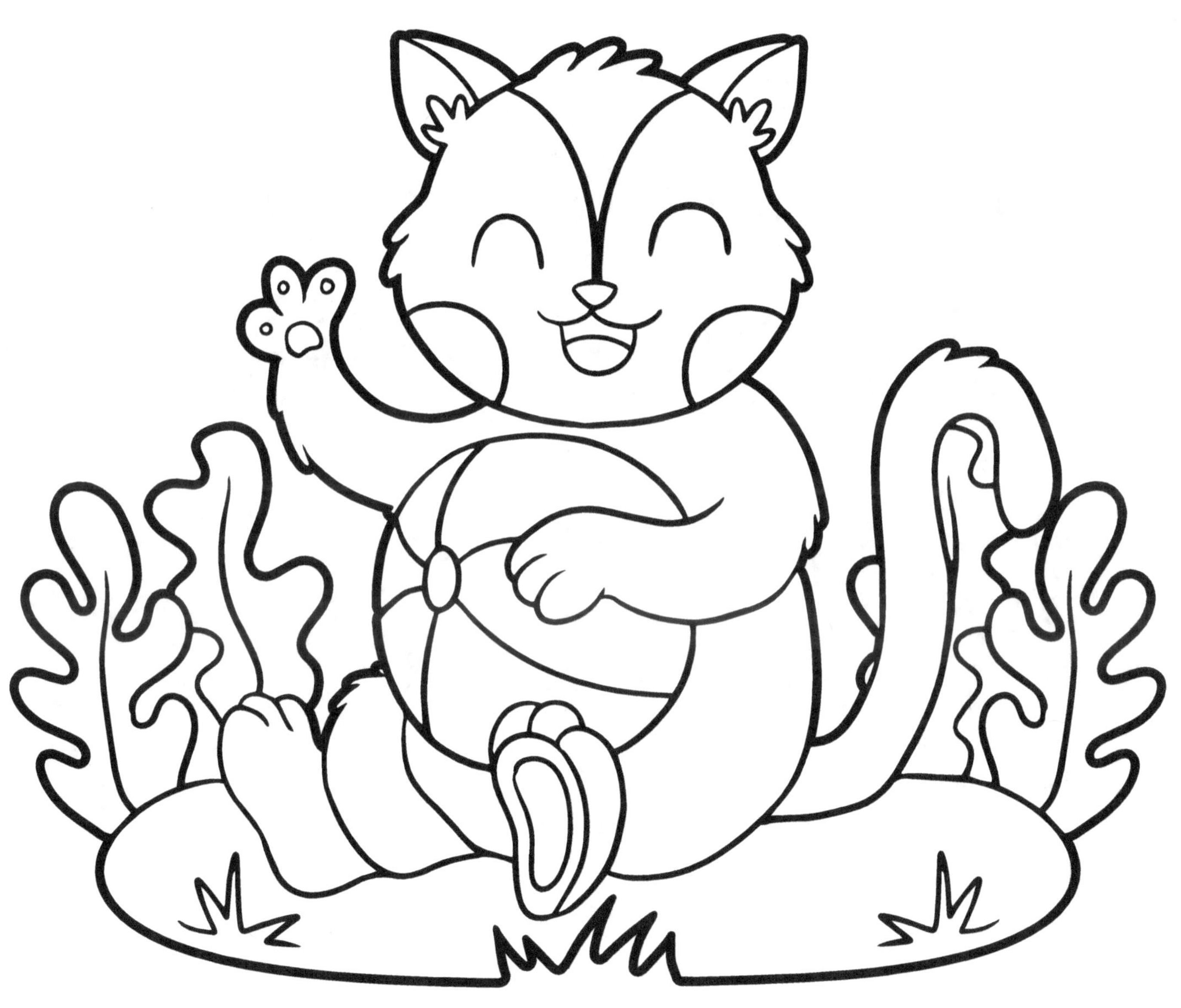

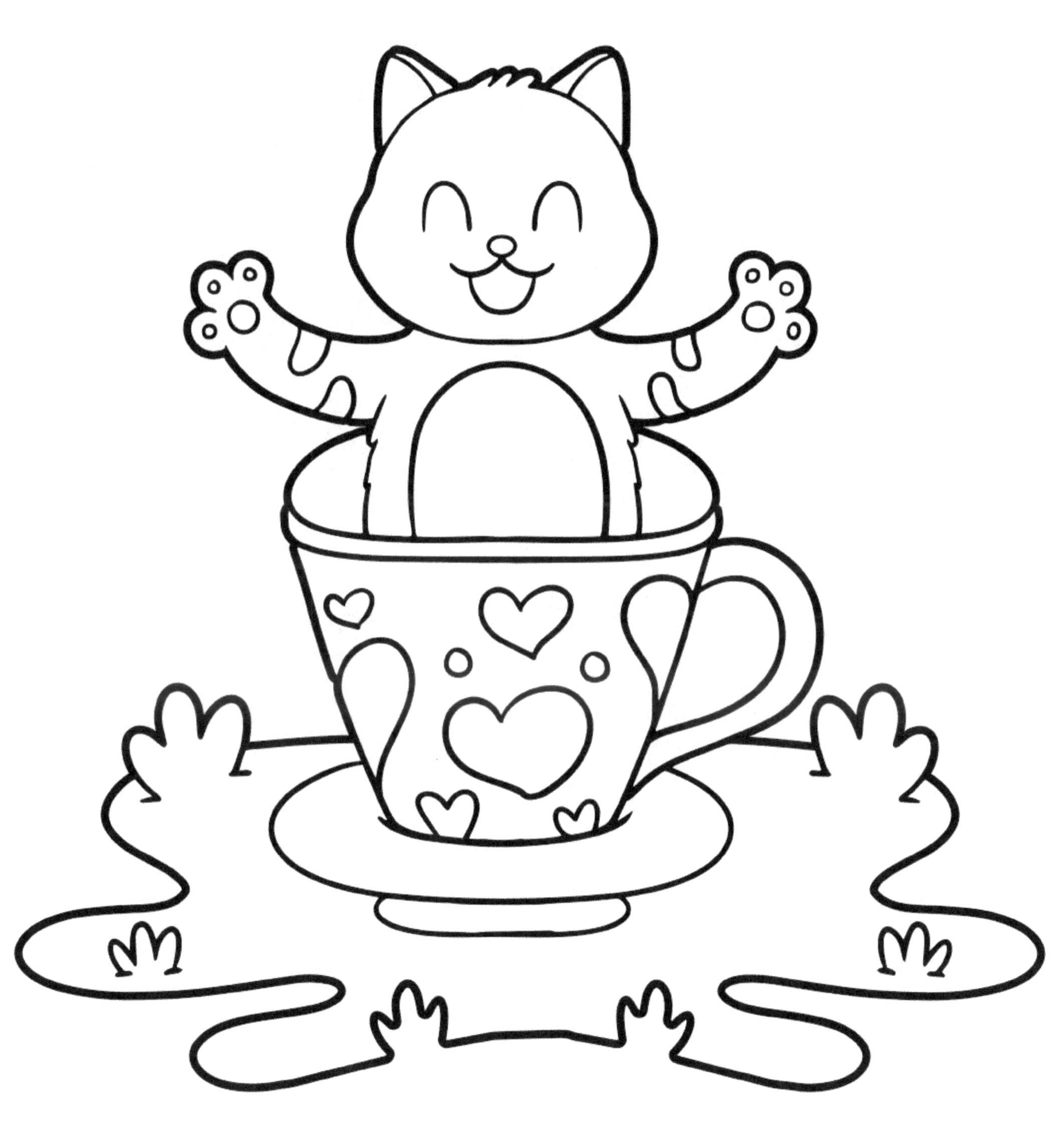

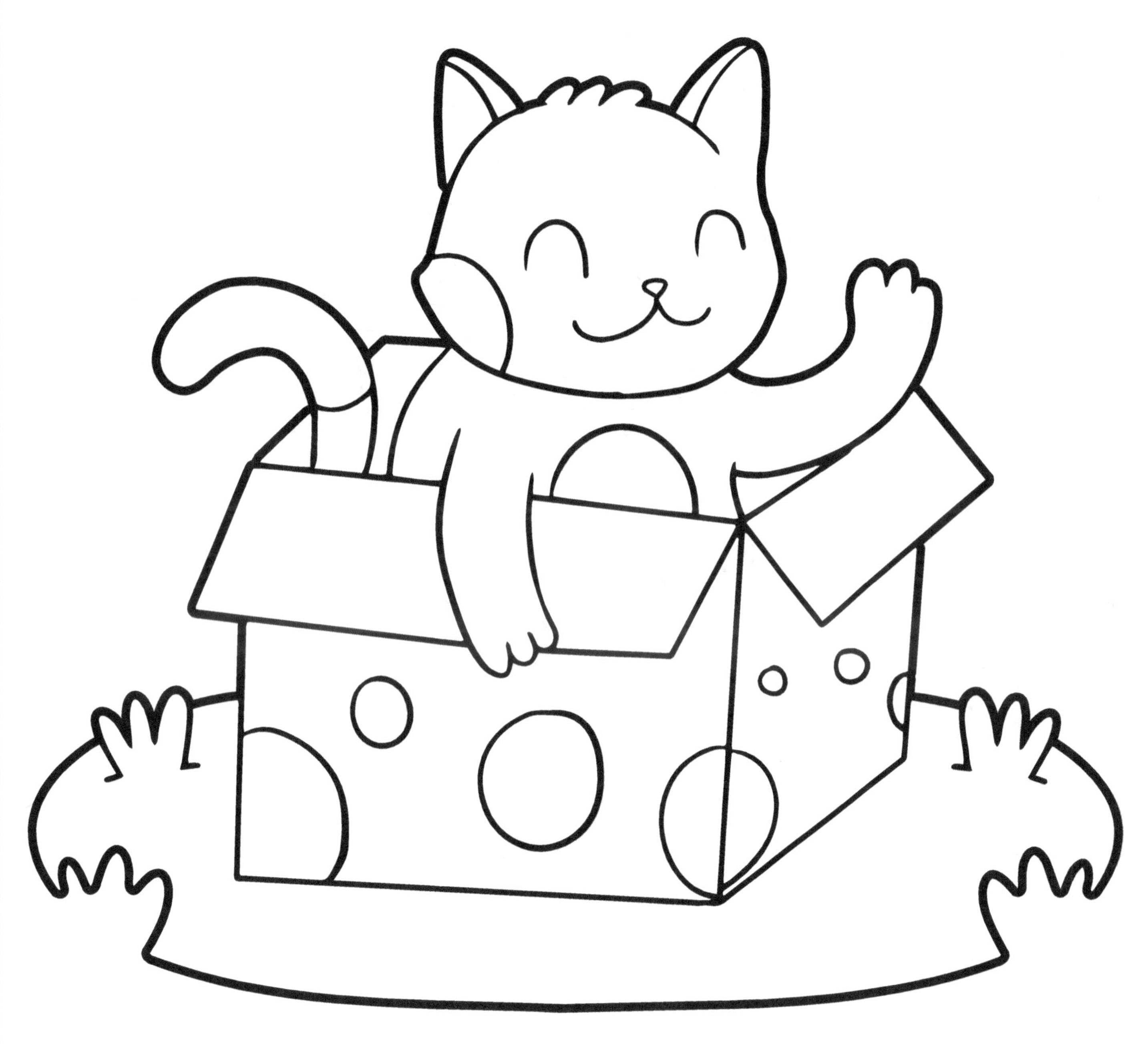

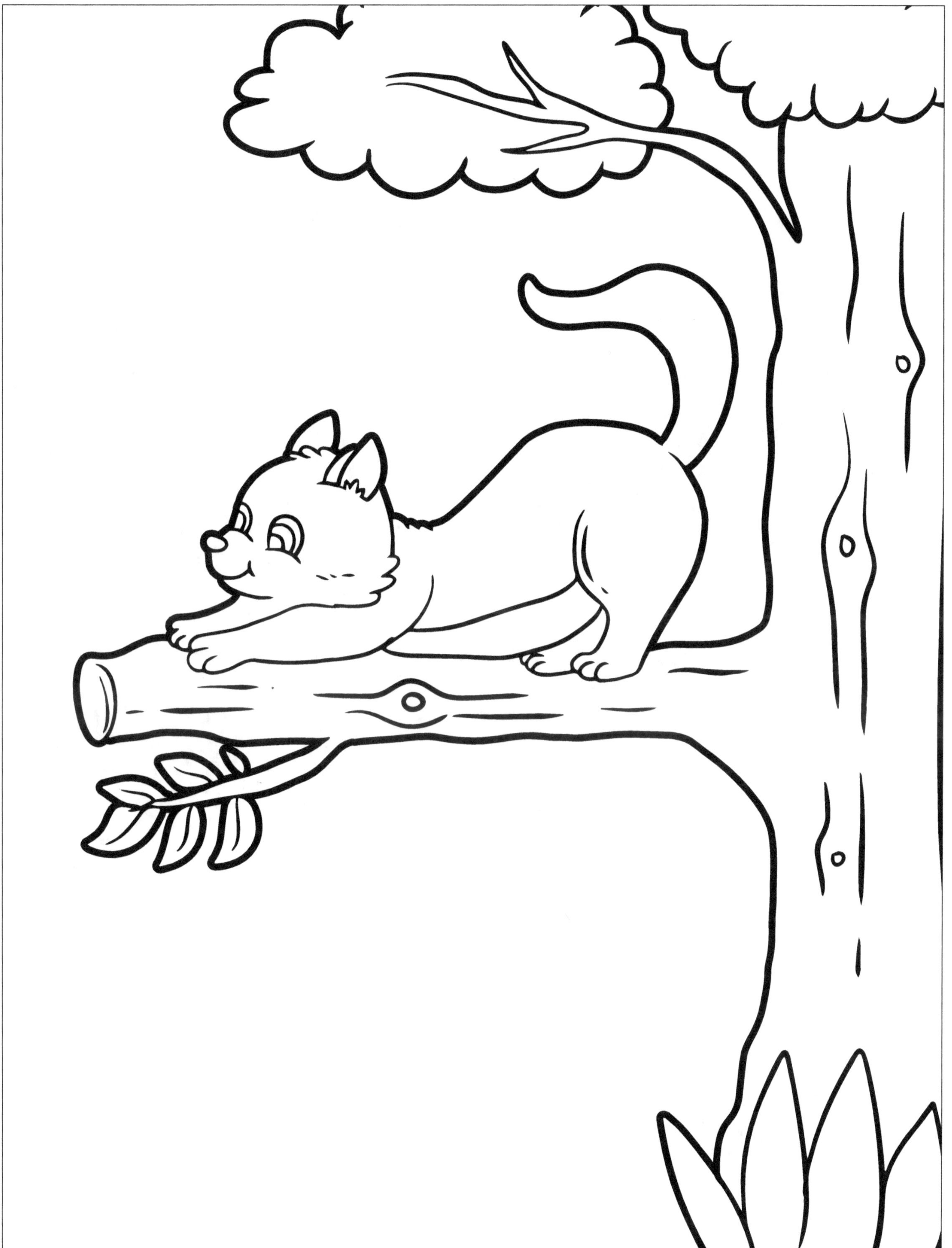

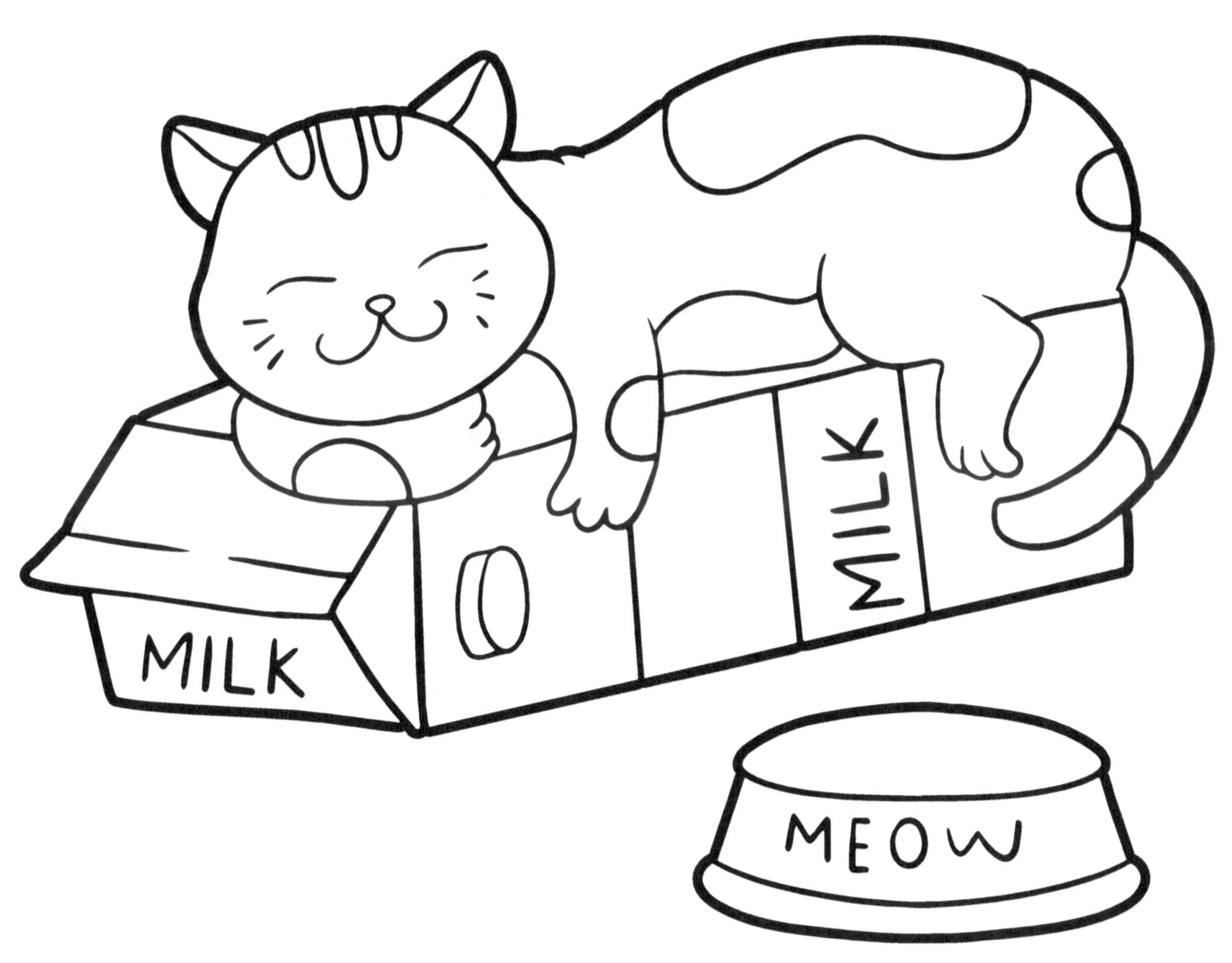
MILK
MILK
MEOW

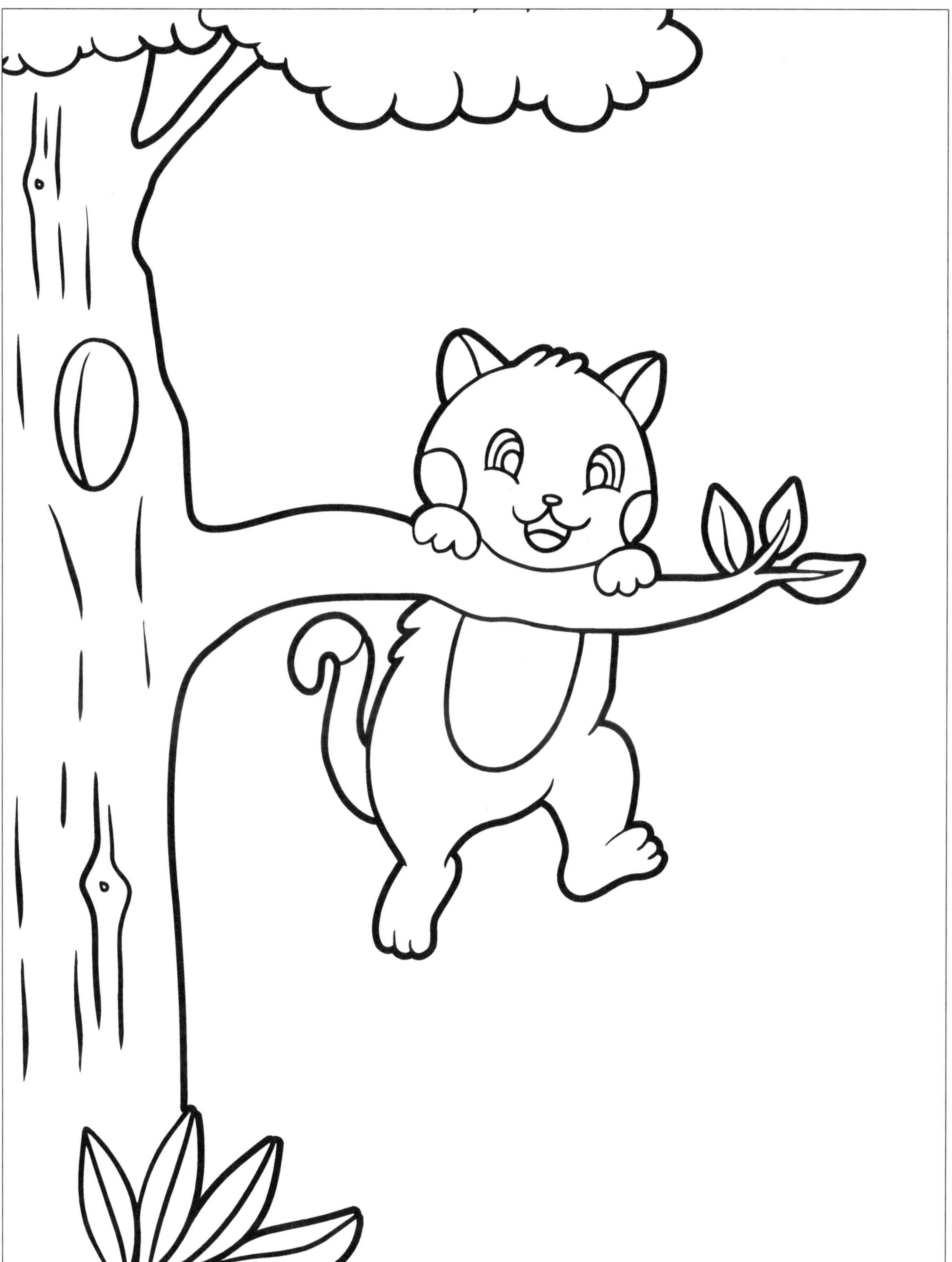

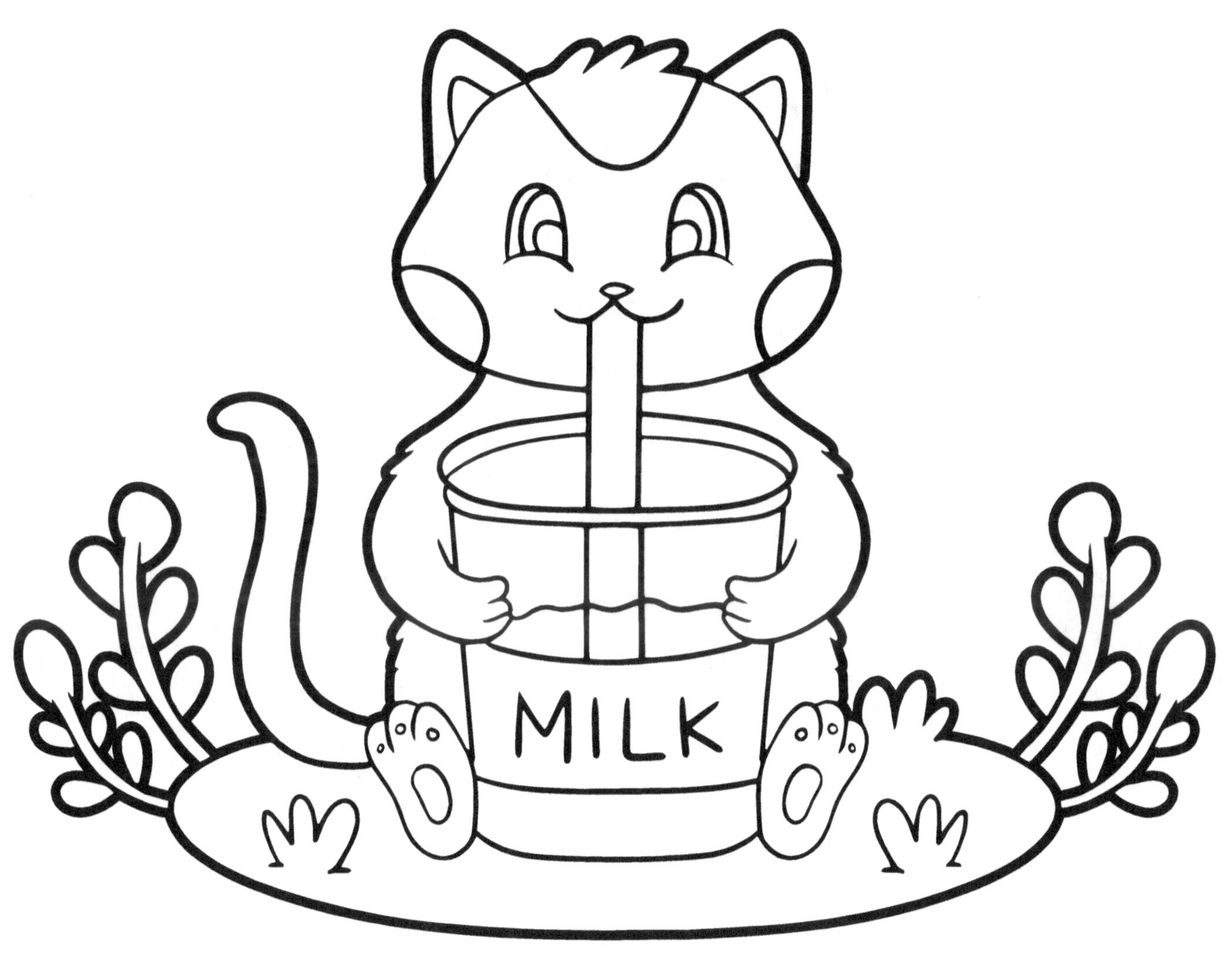
MILK

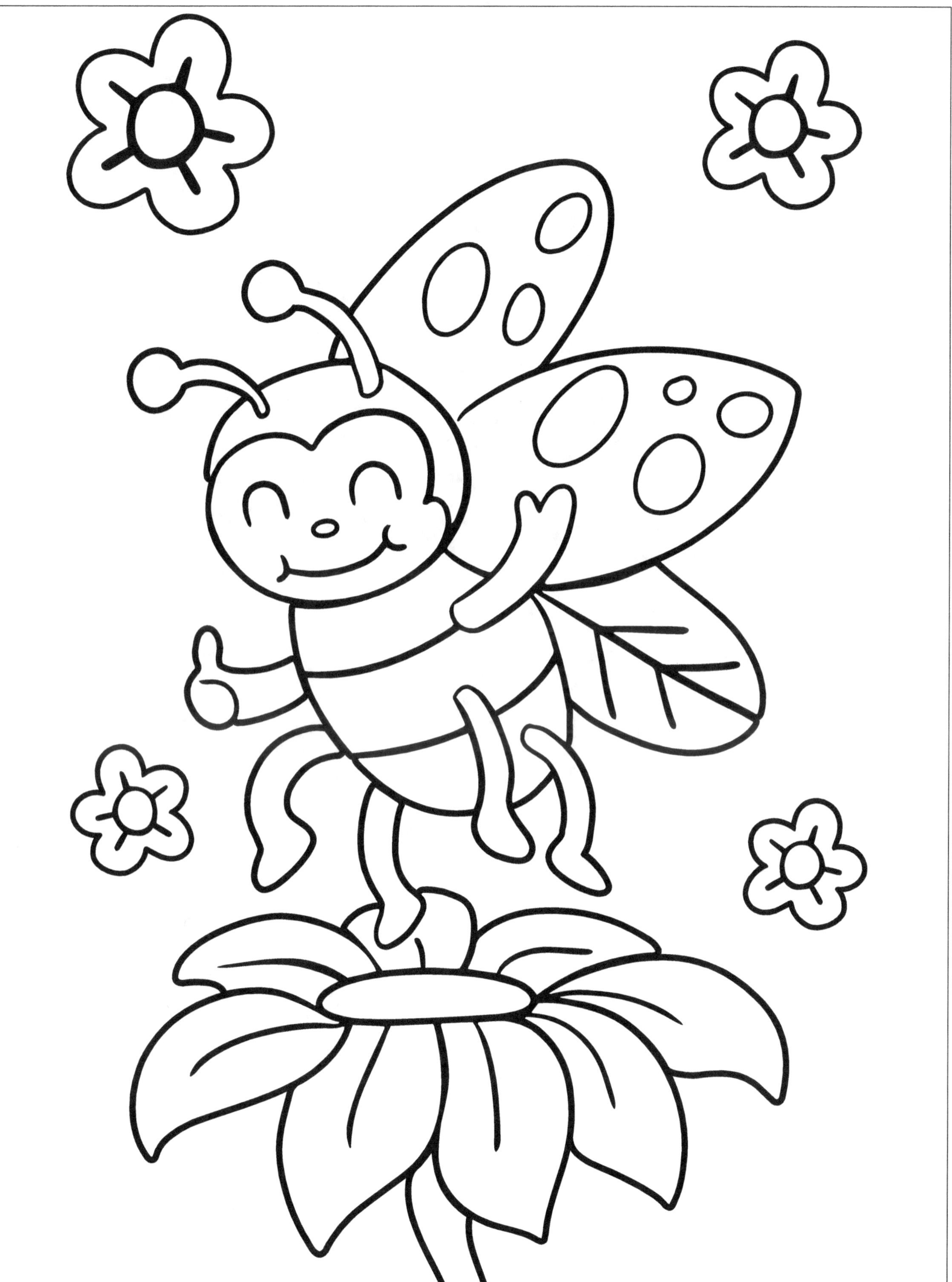

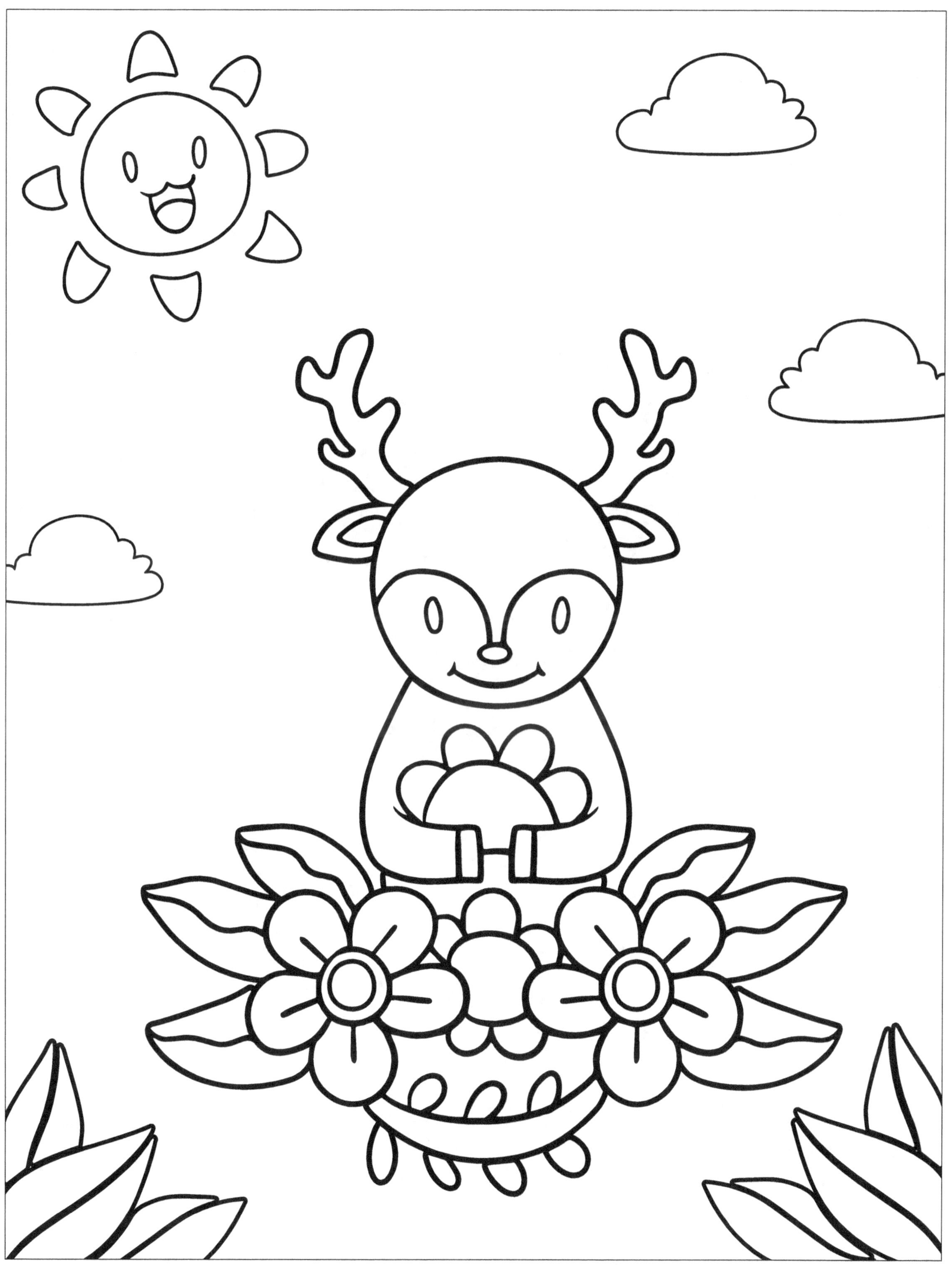

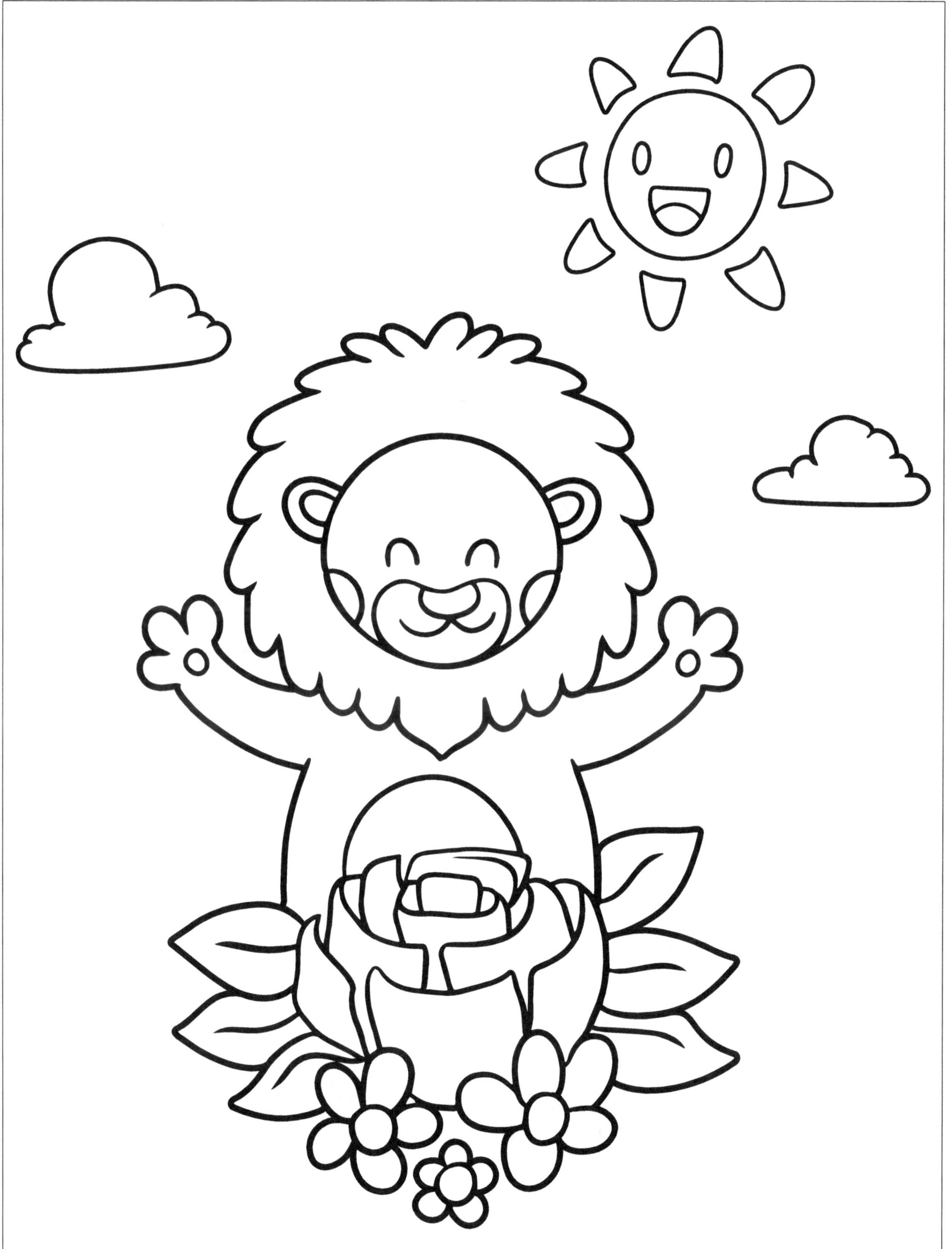

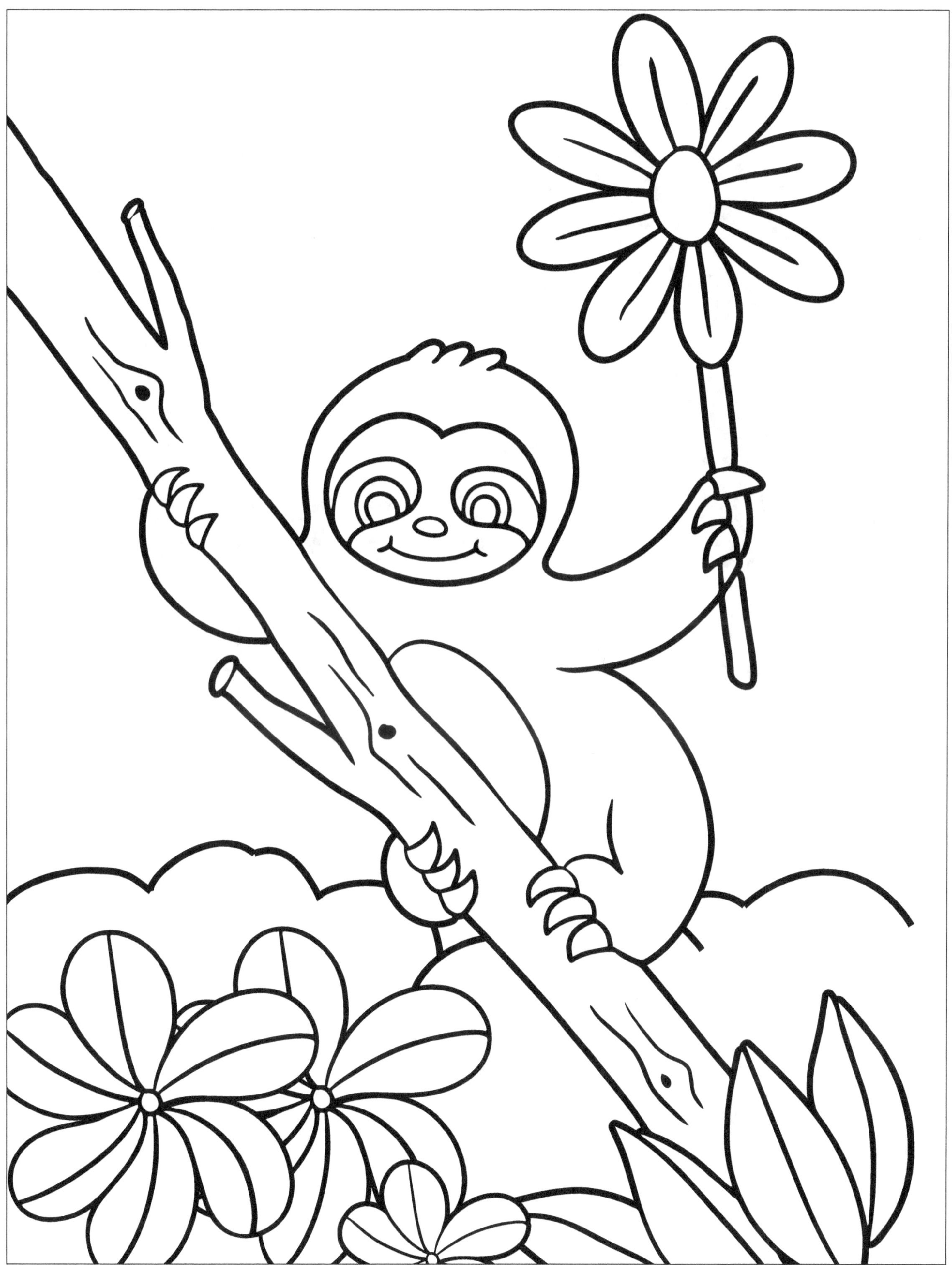

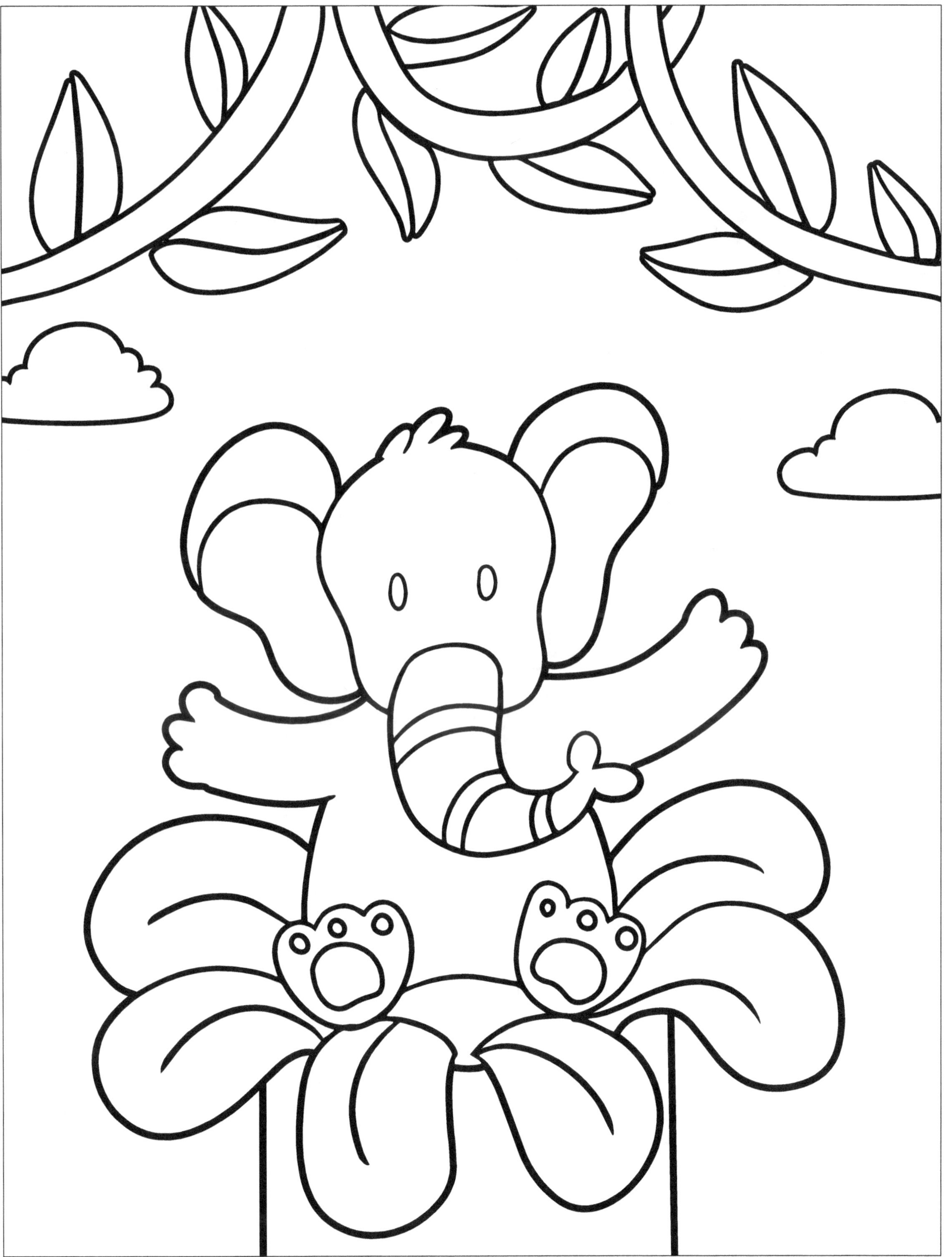

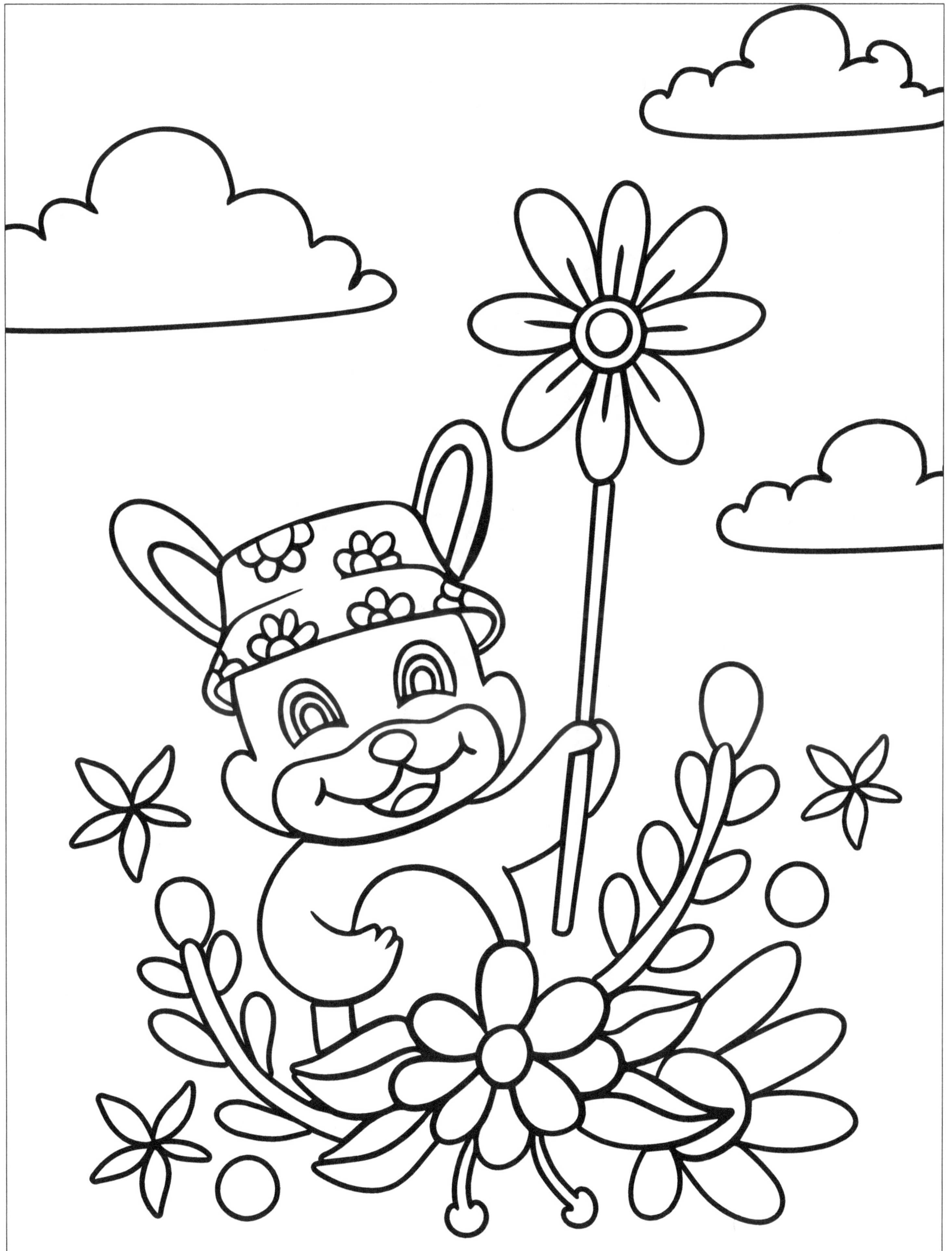

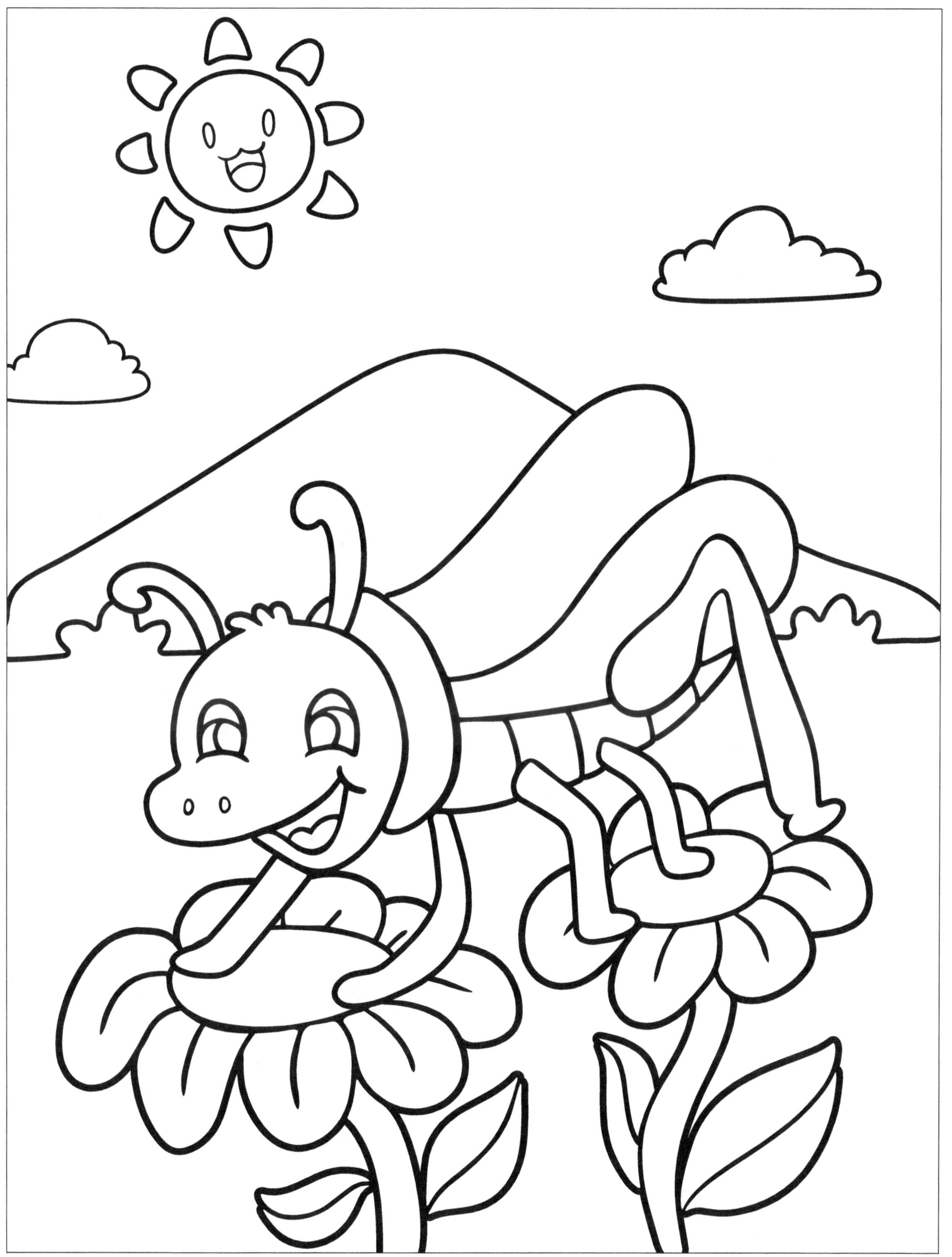

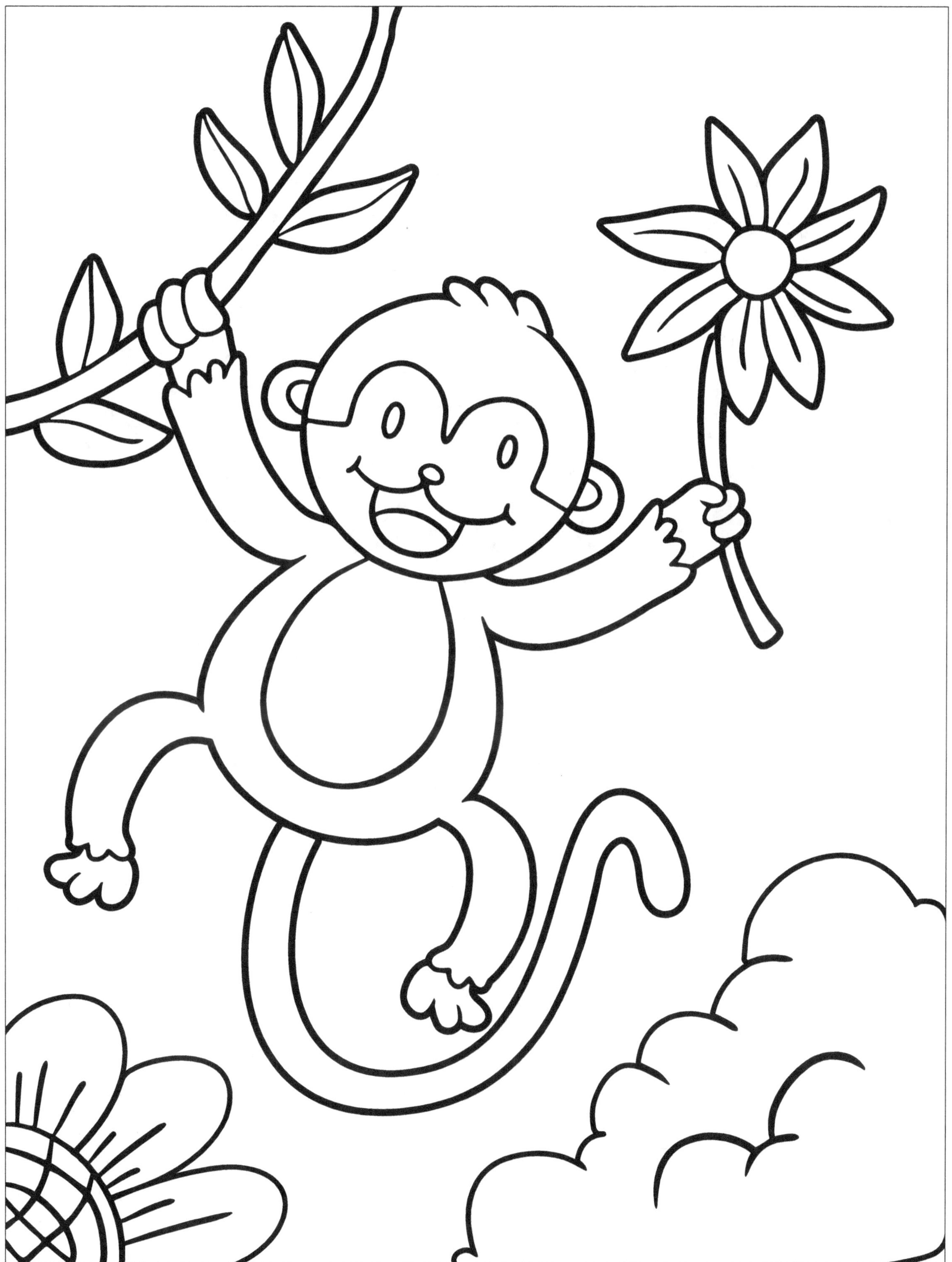

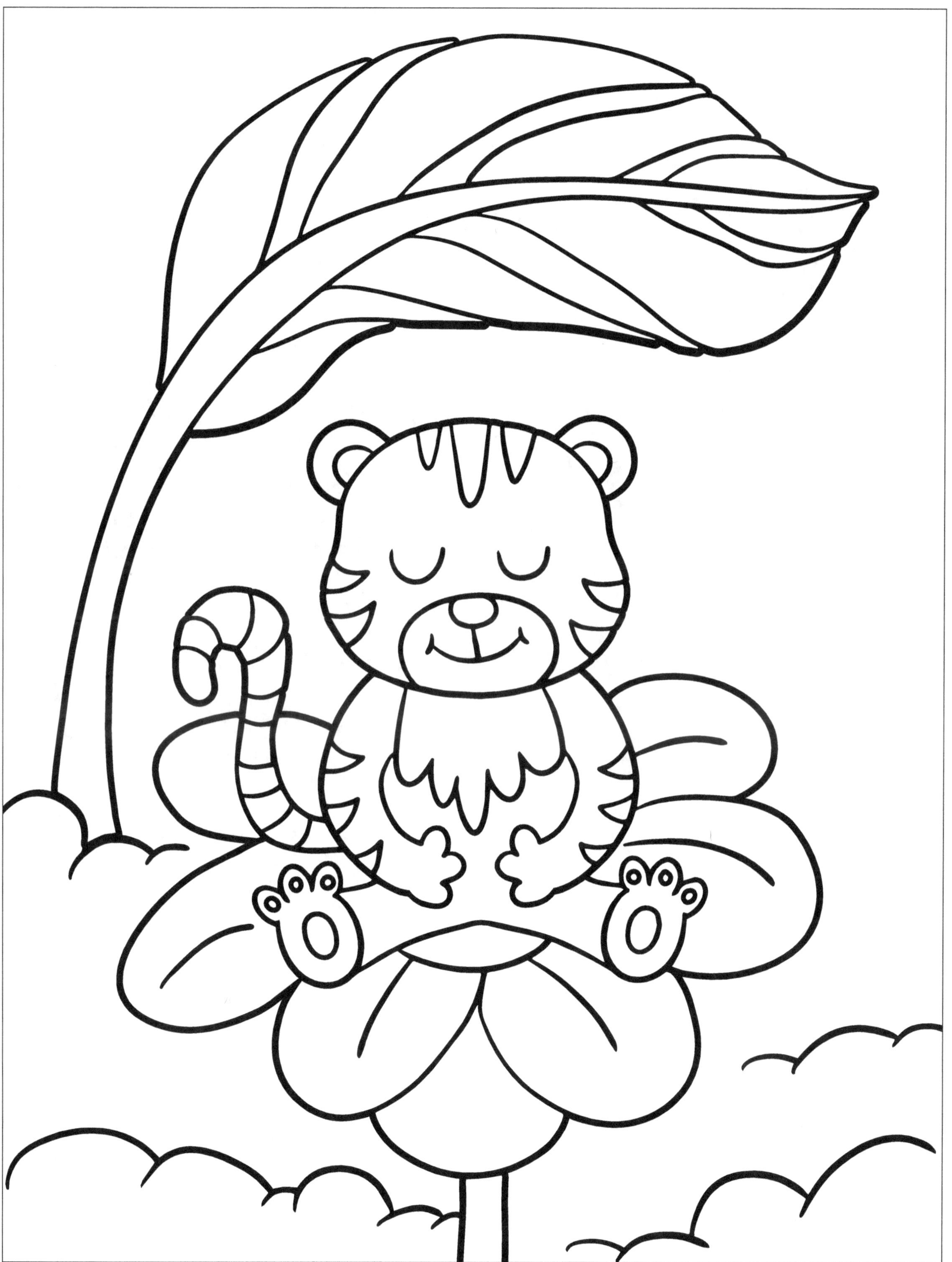

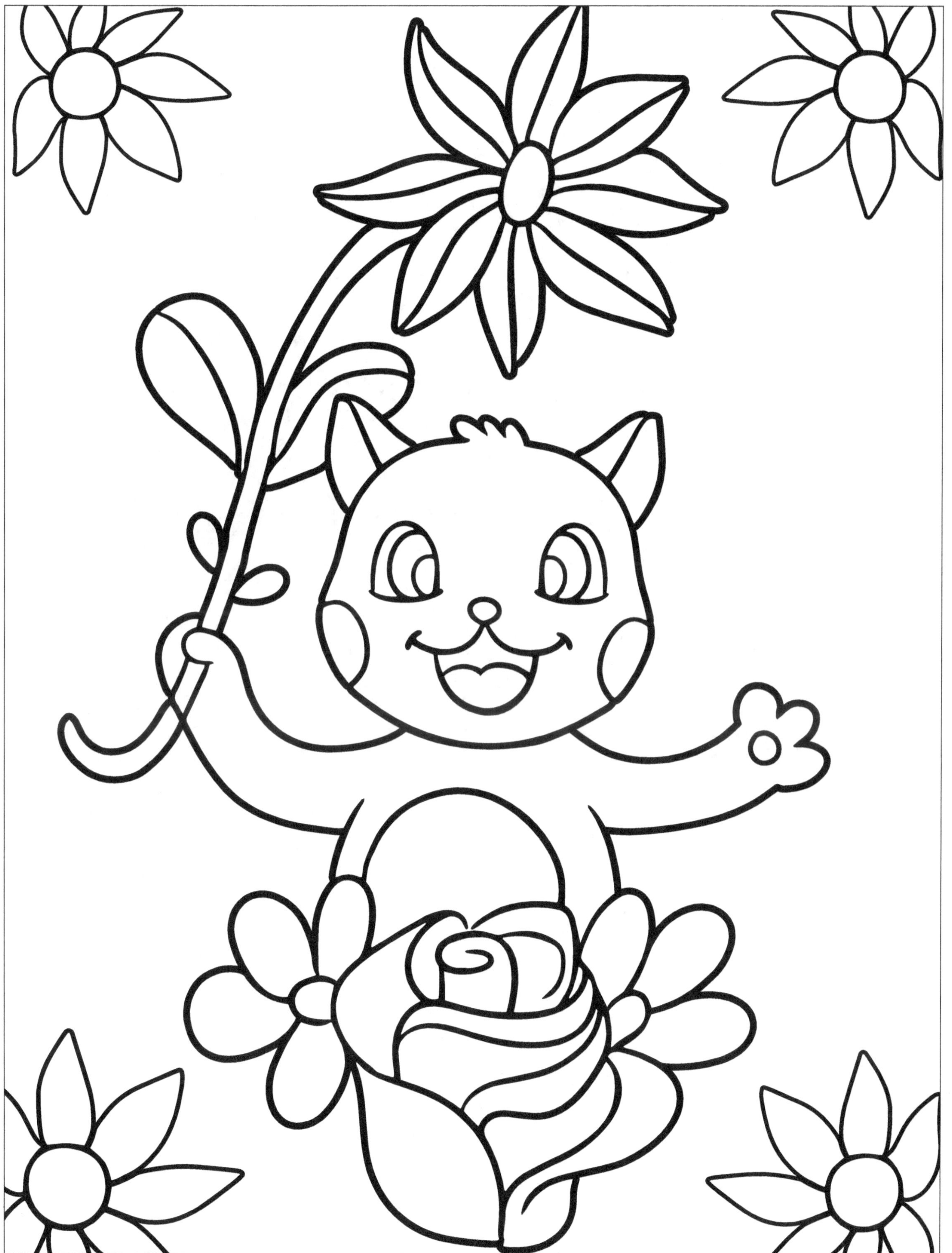

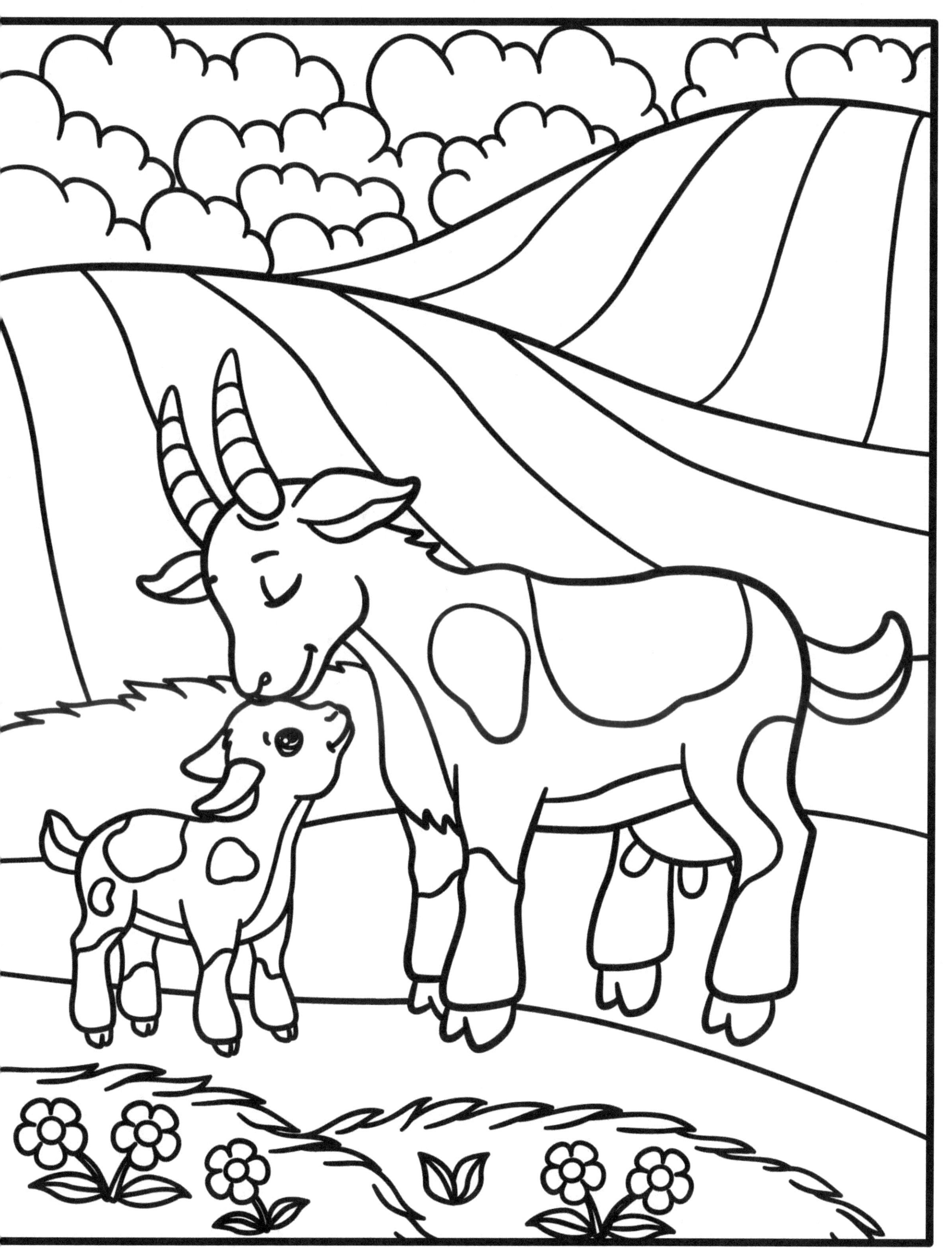

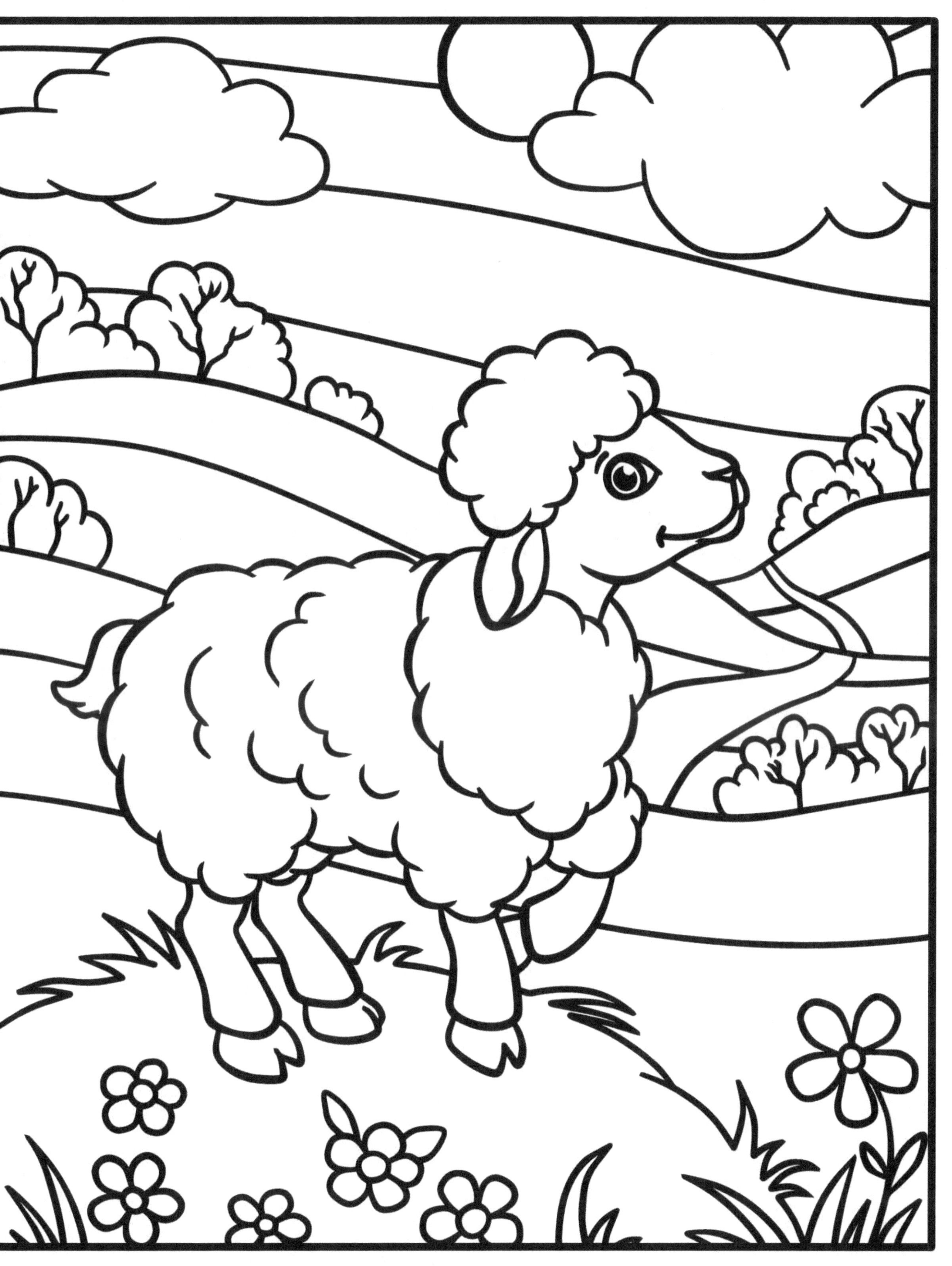

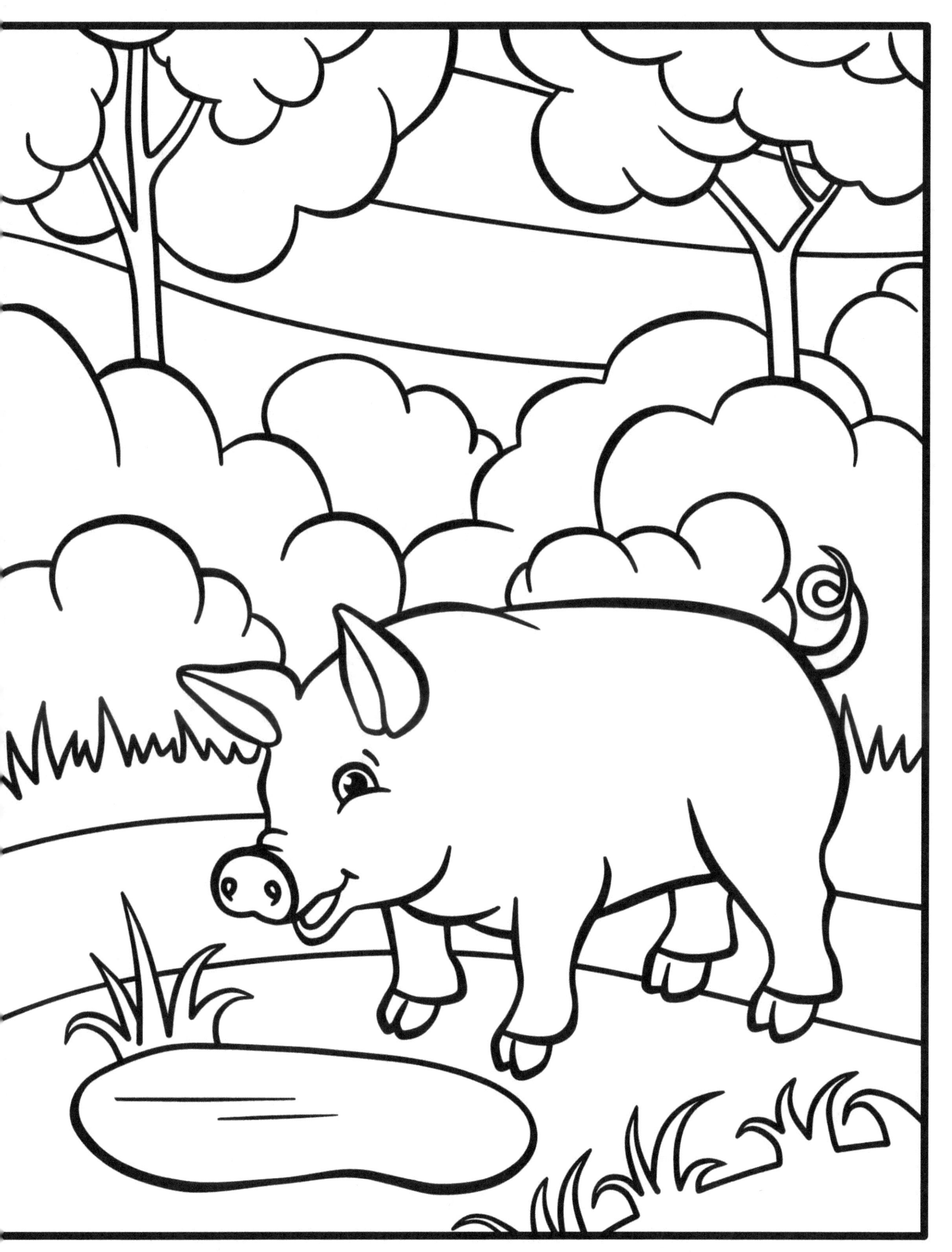

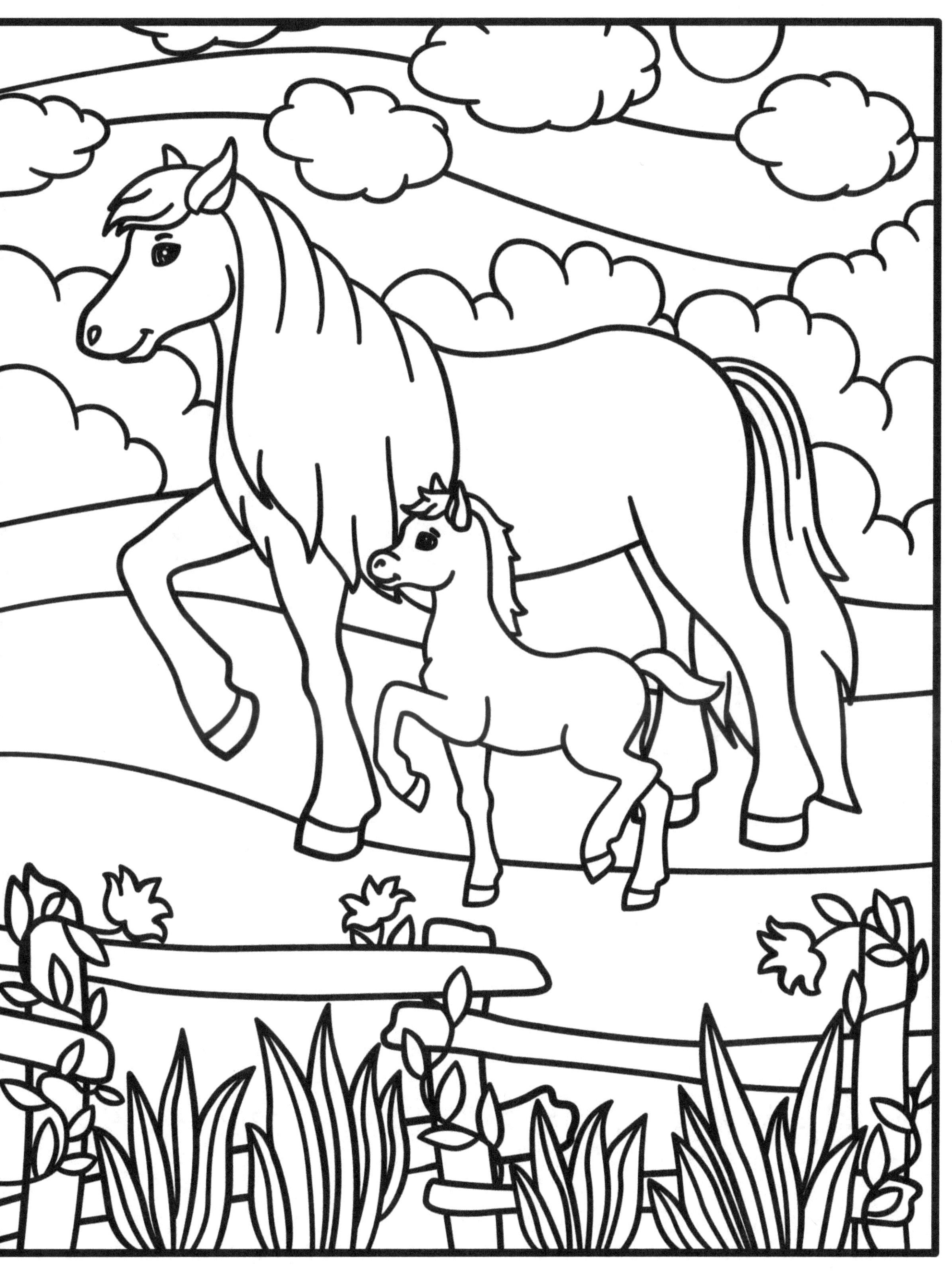

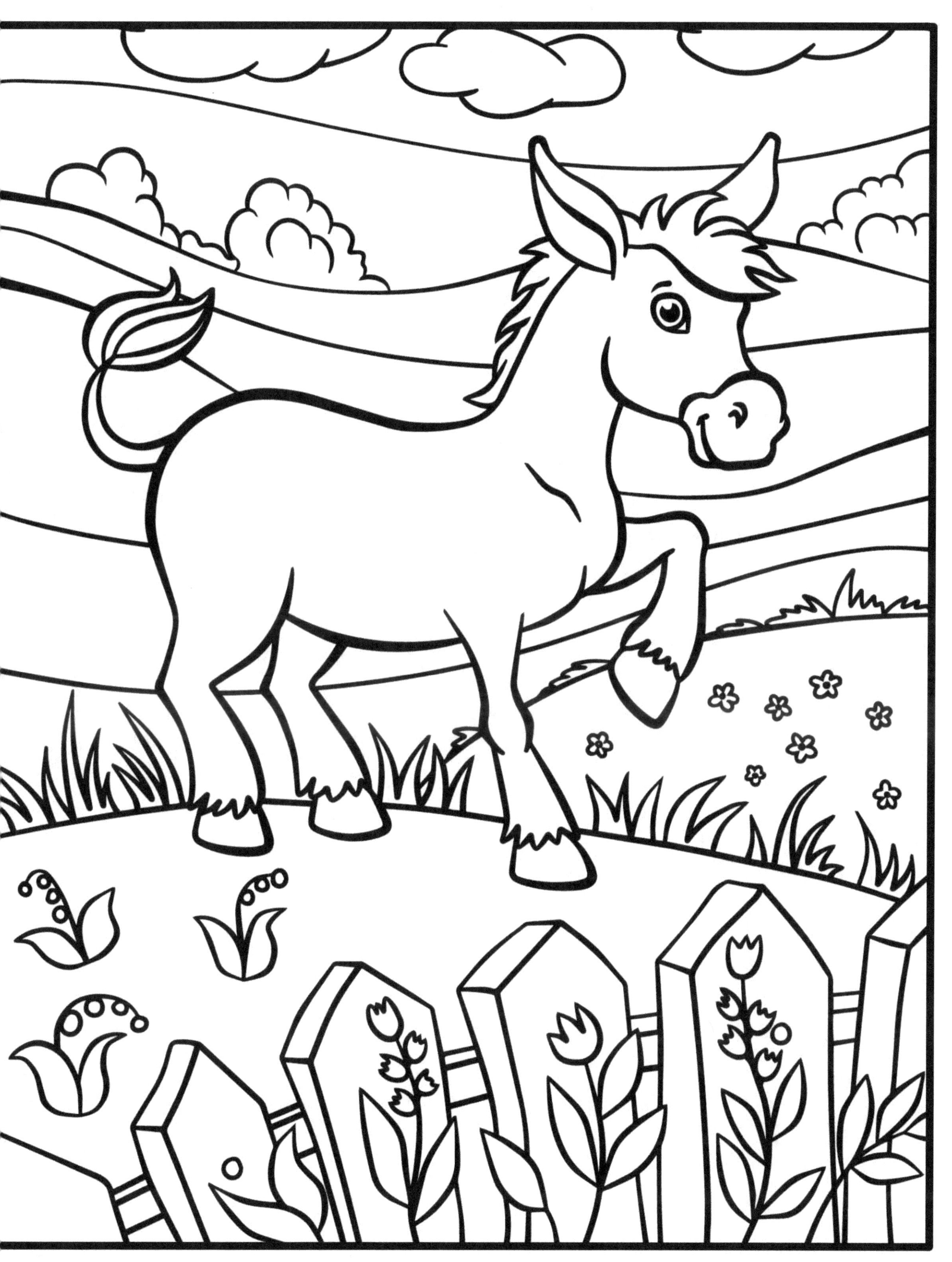

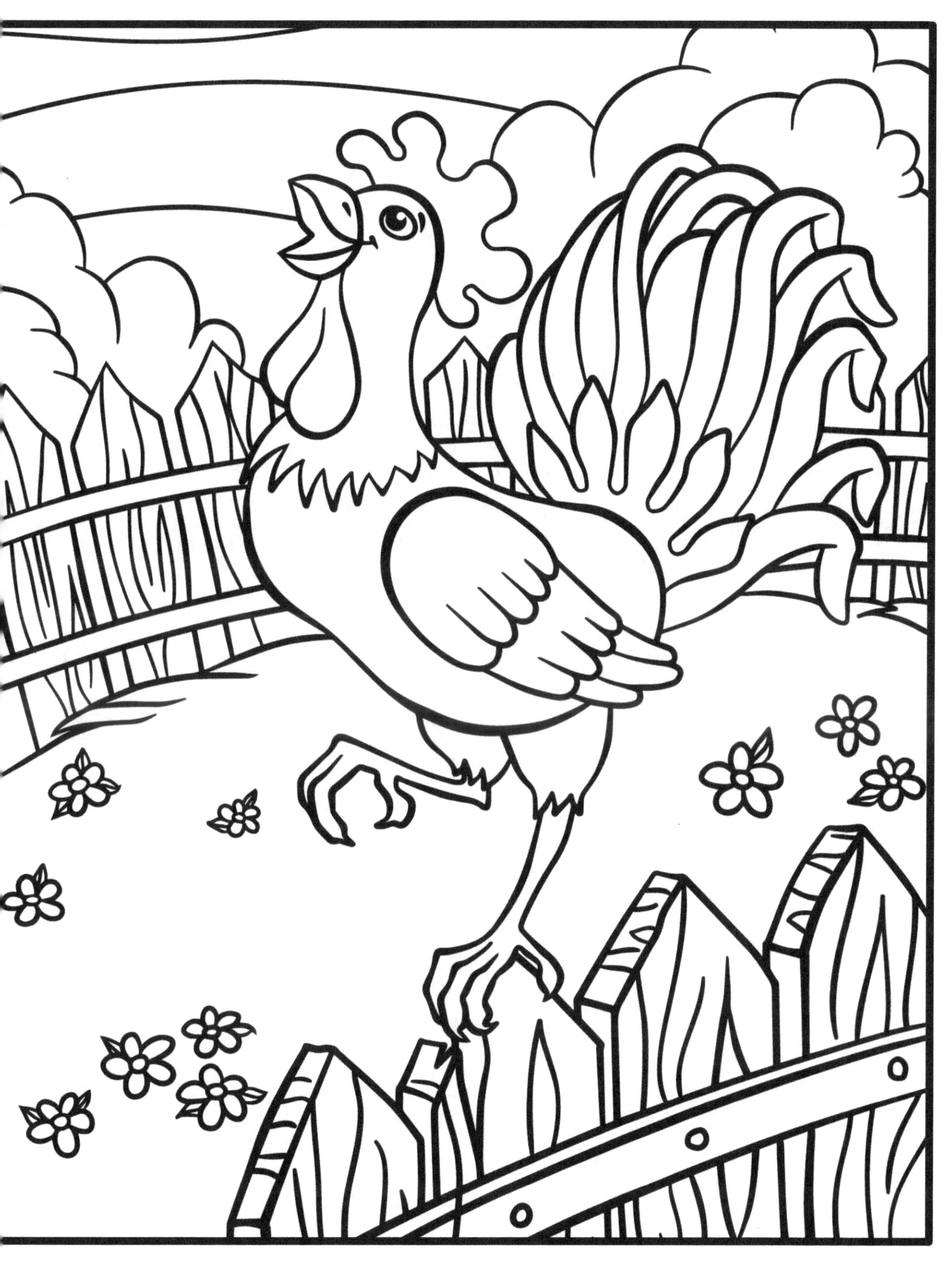

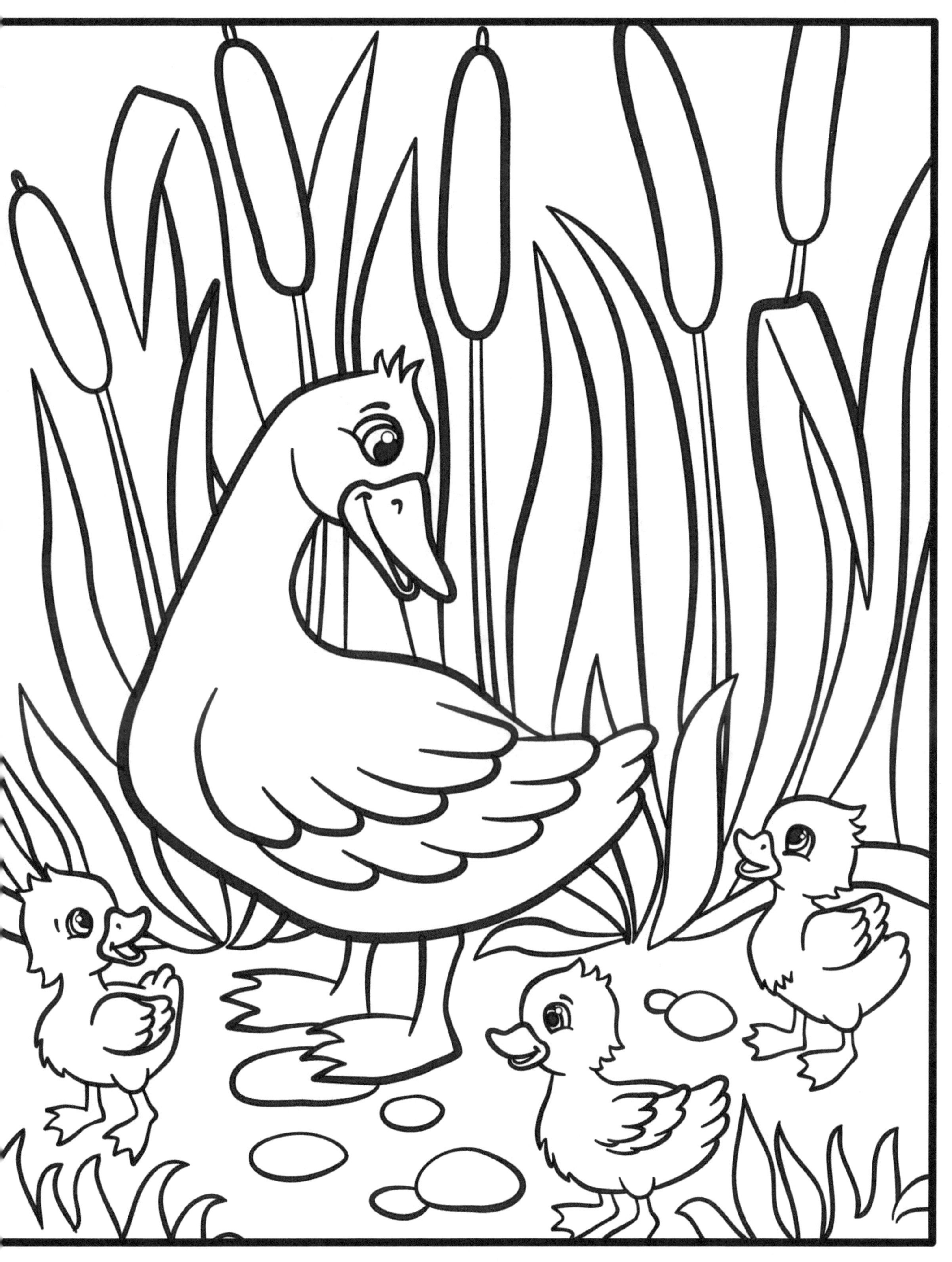

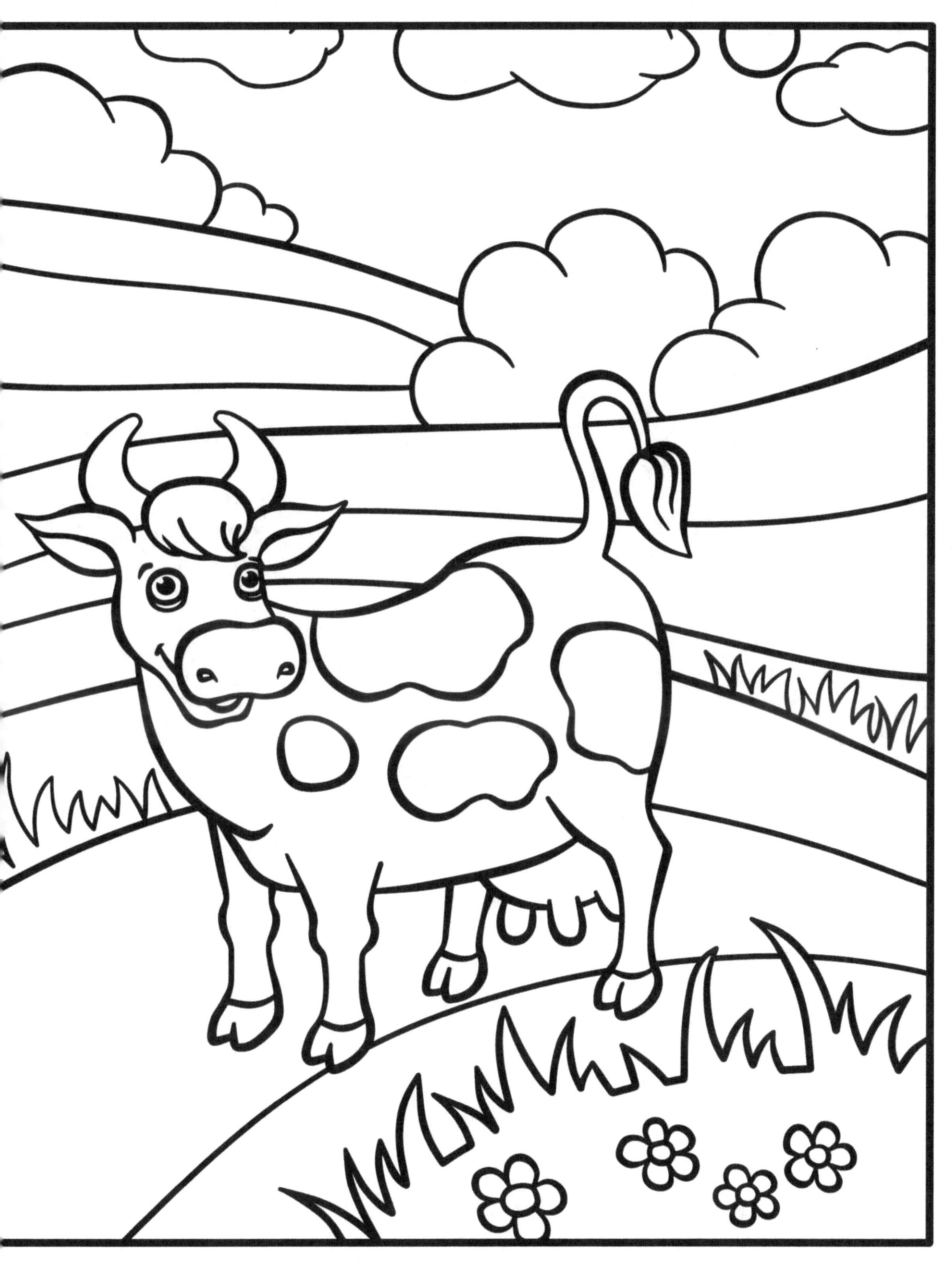

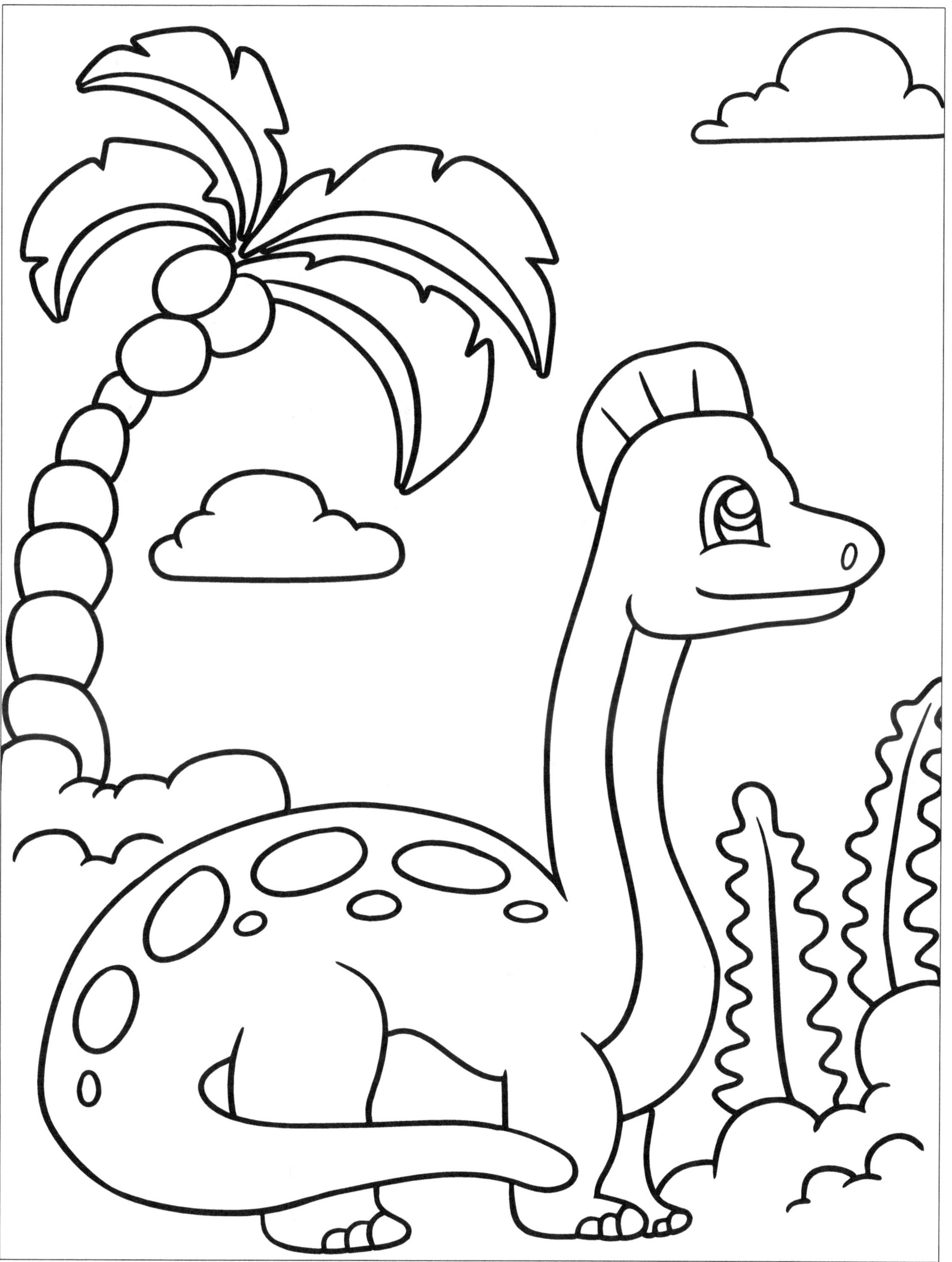

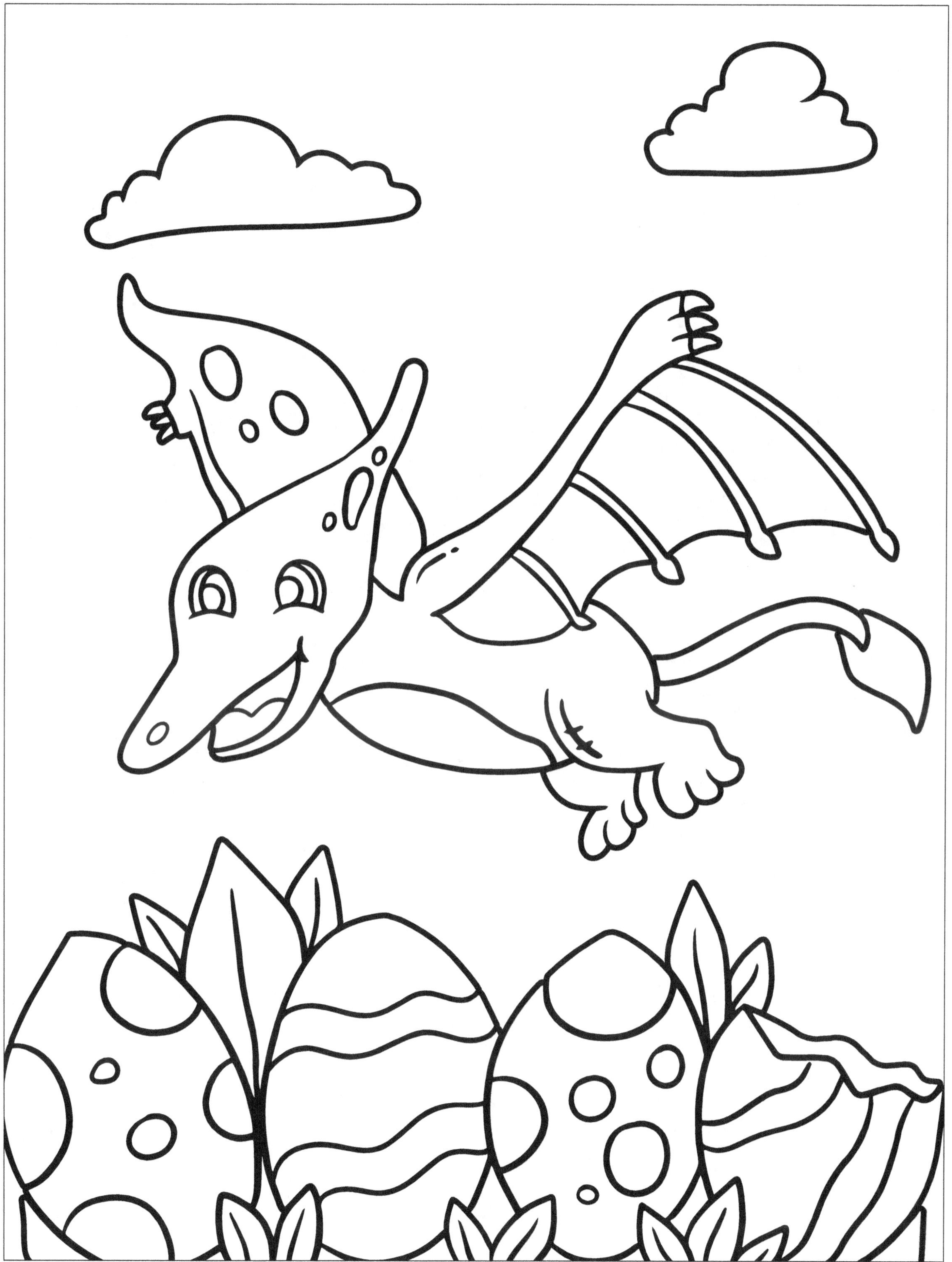

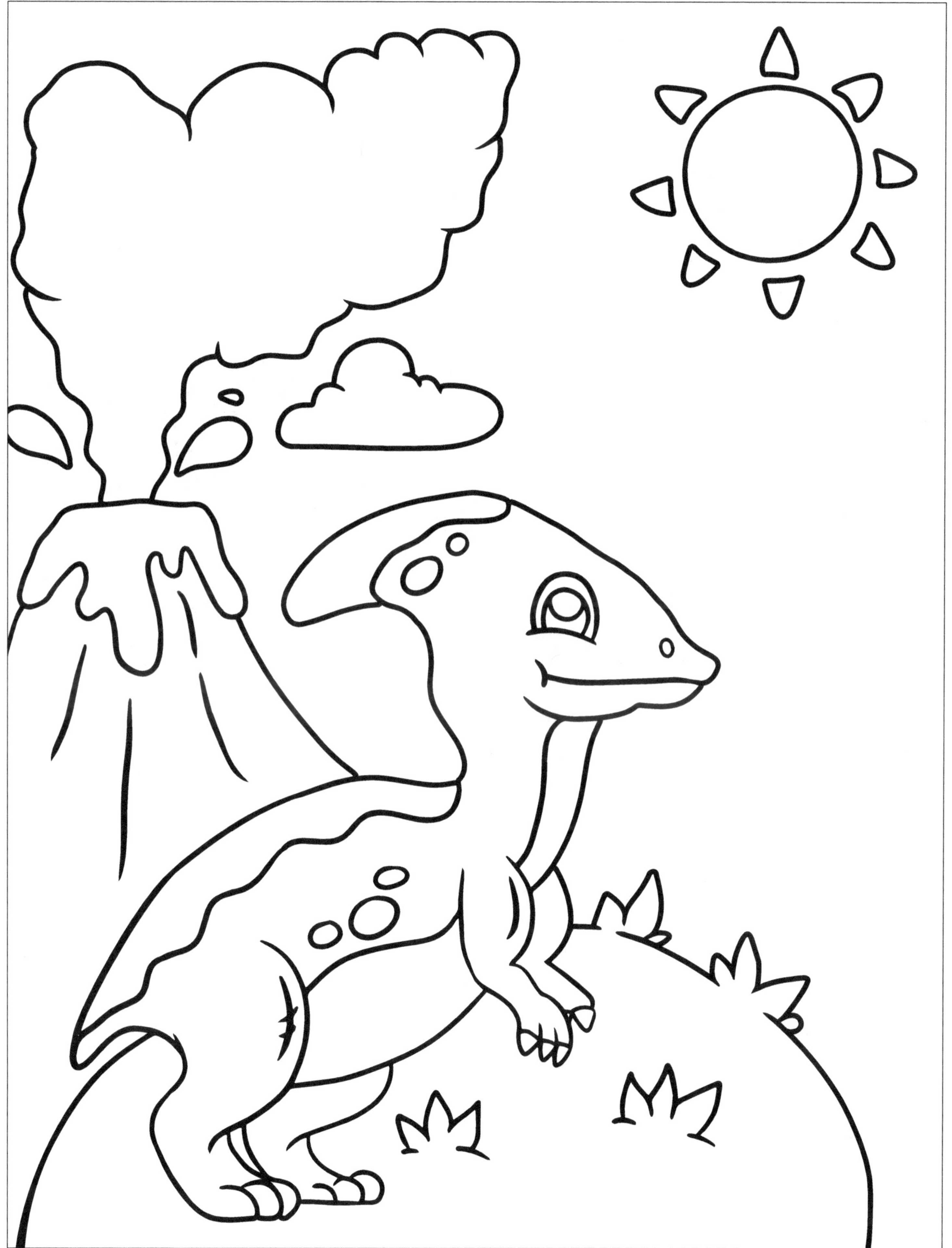

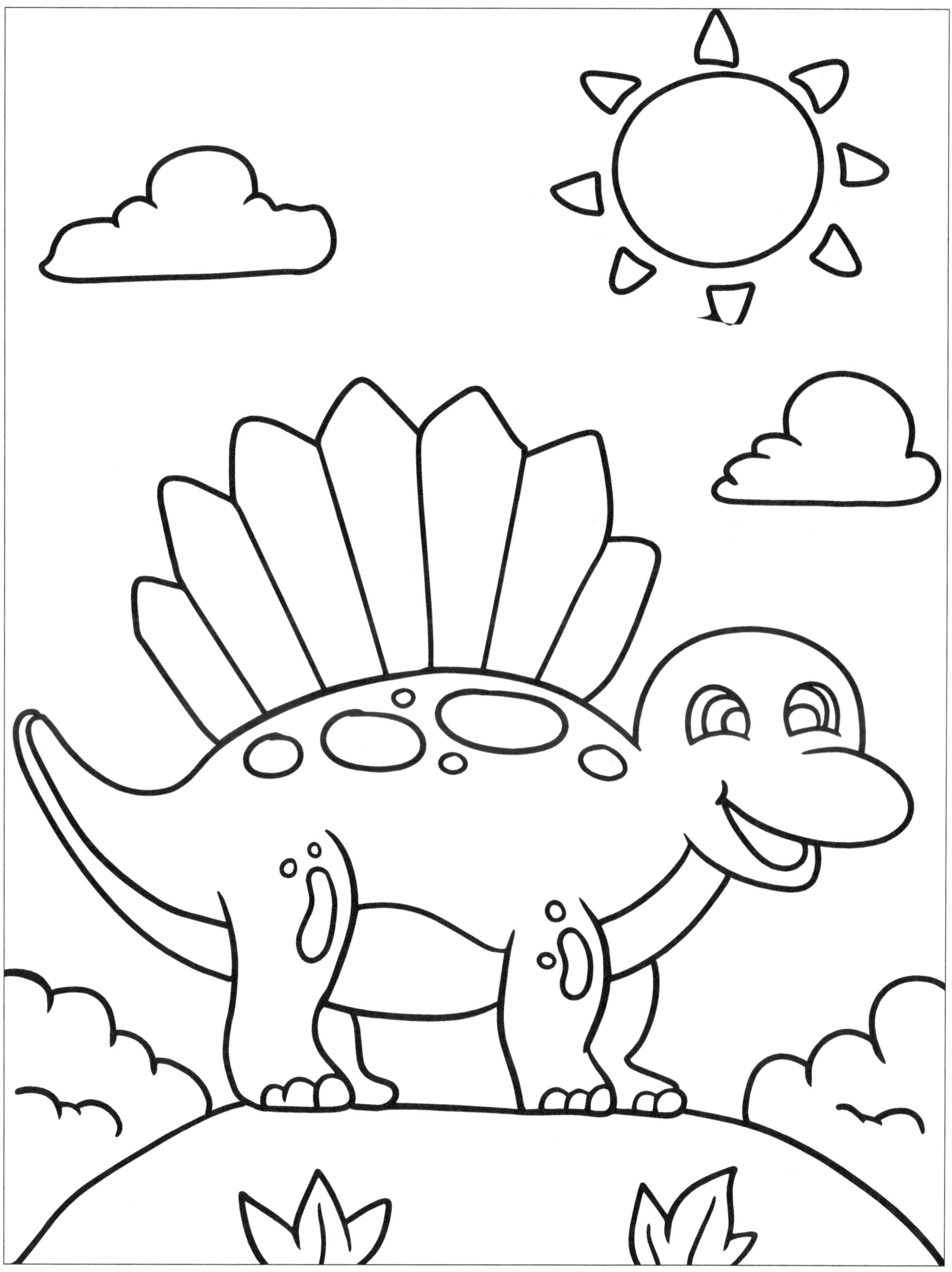

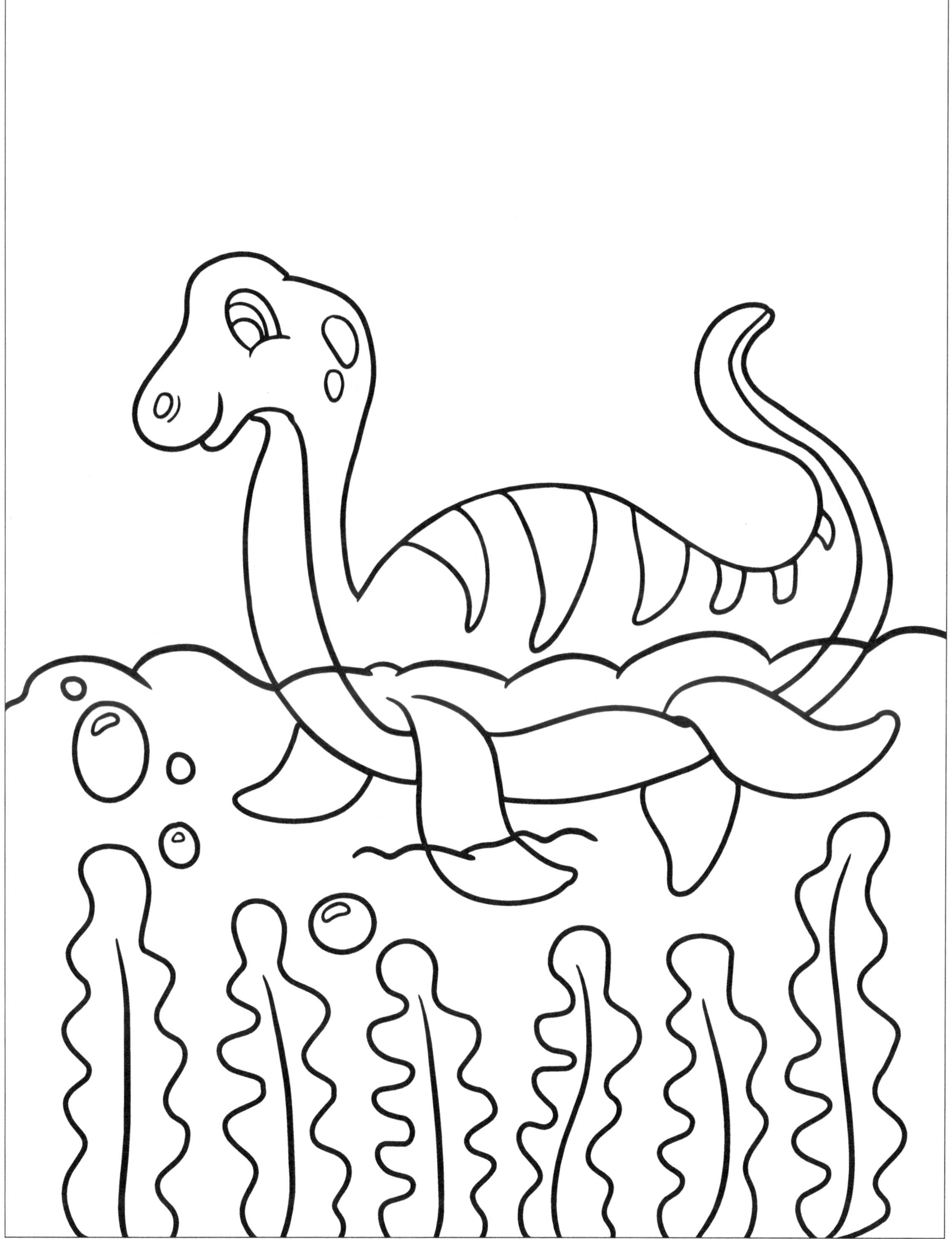

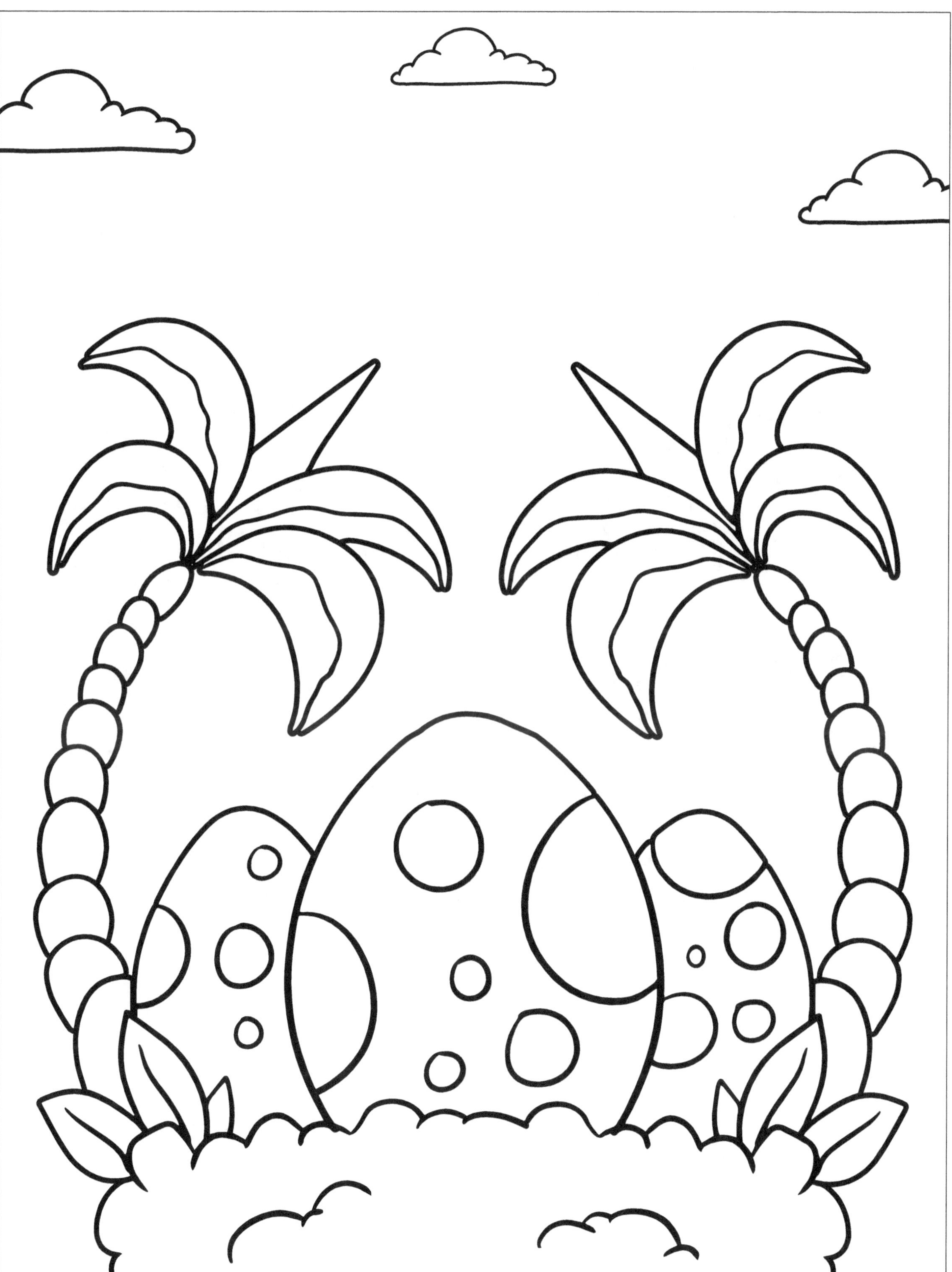

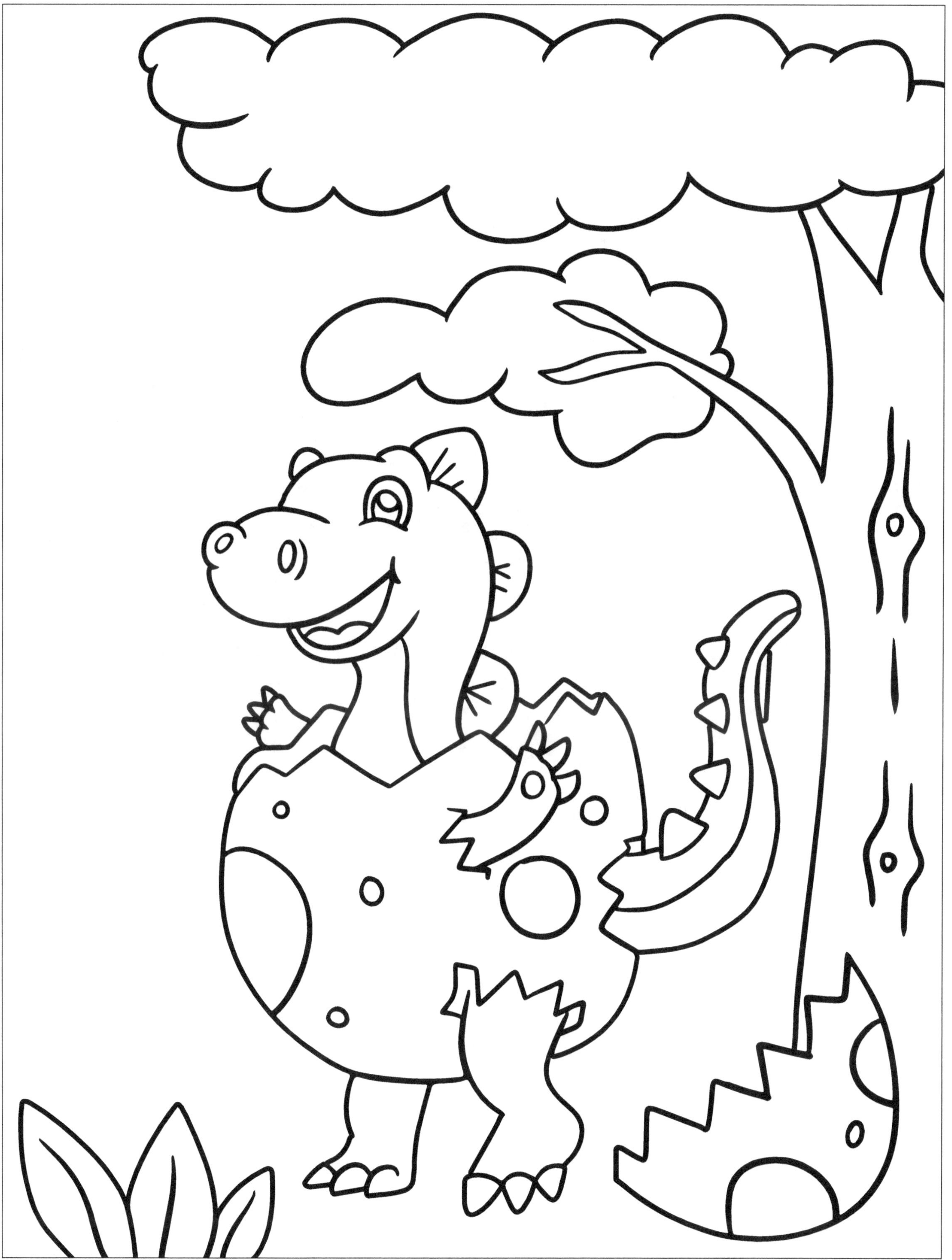

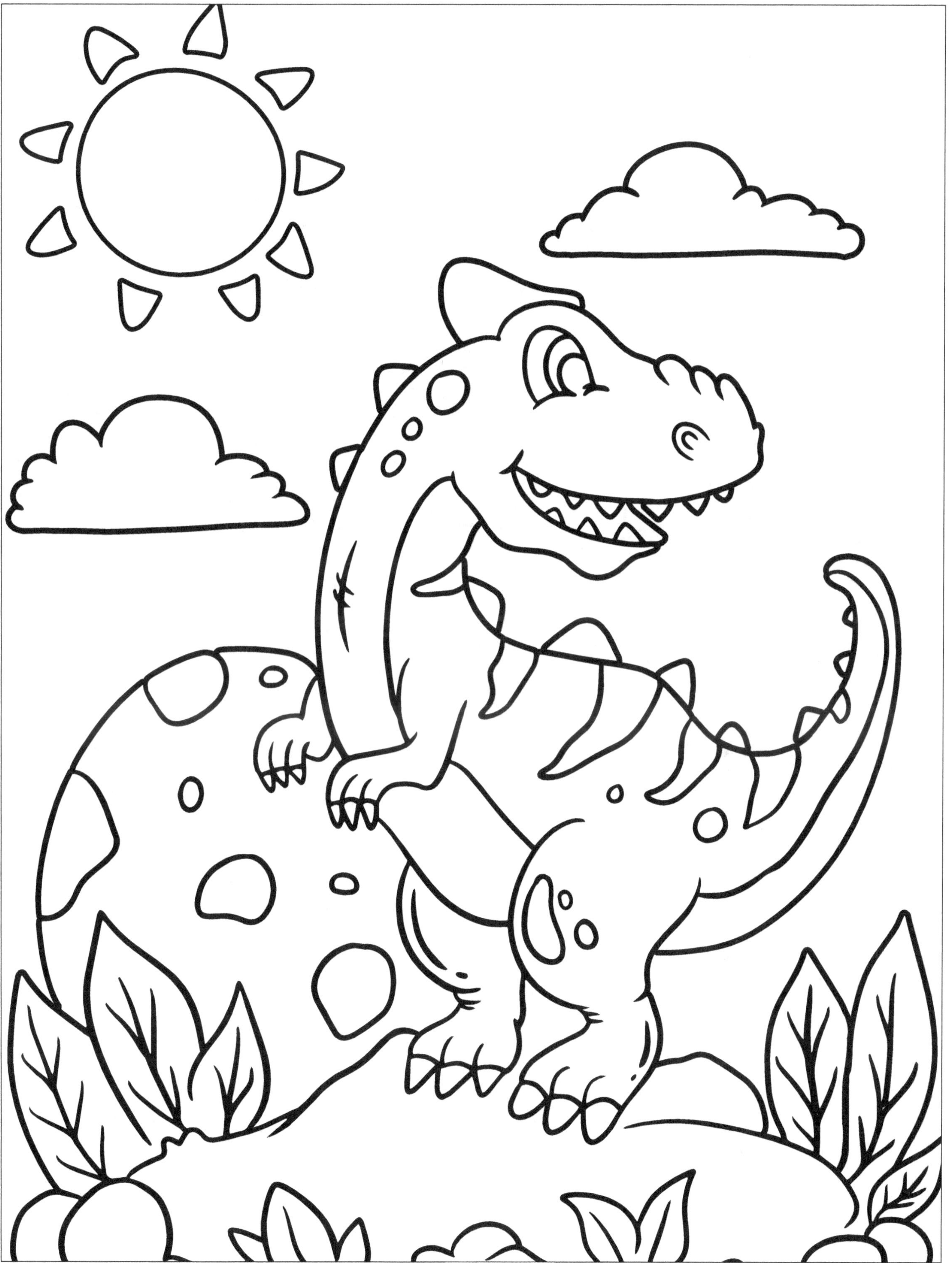

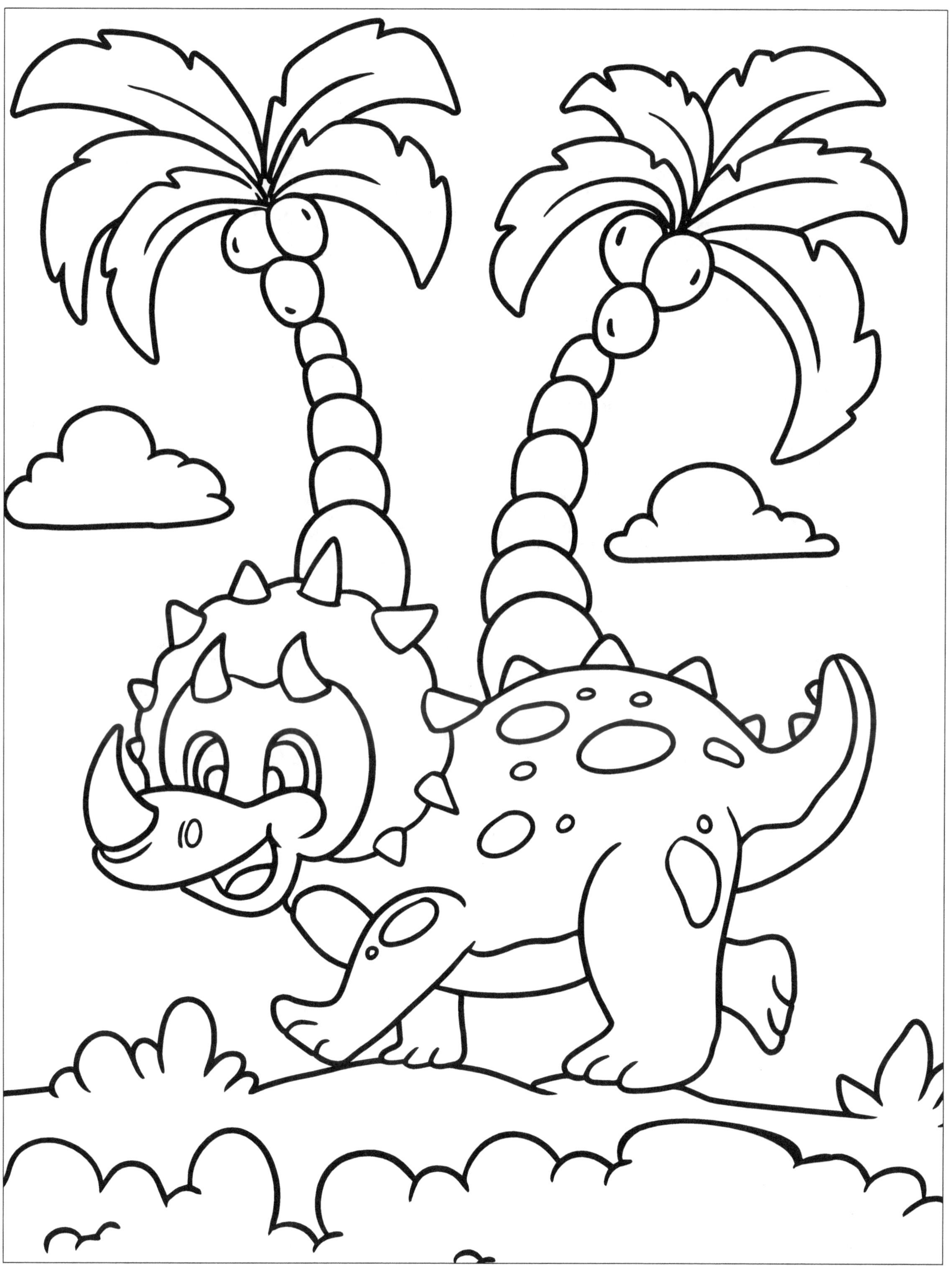

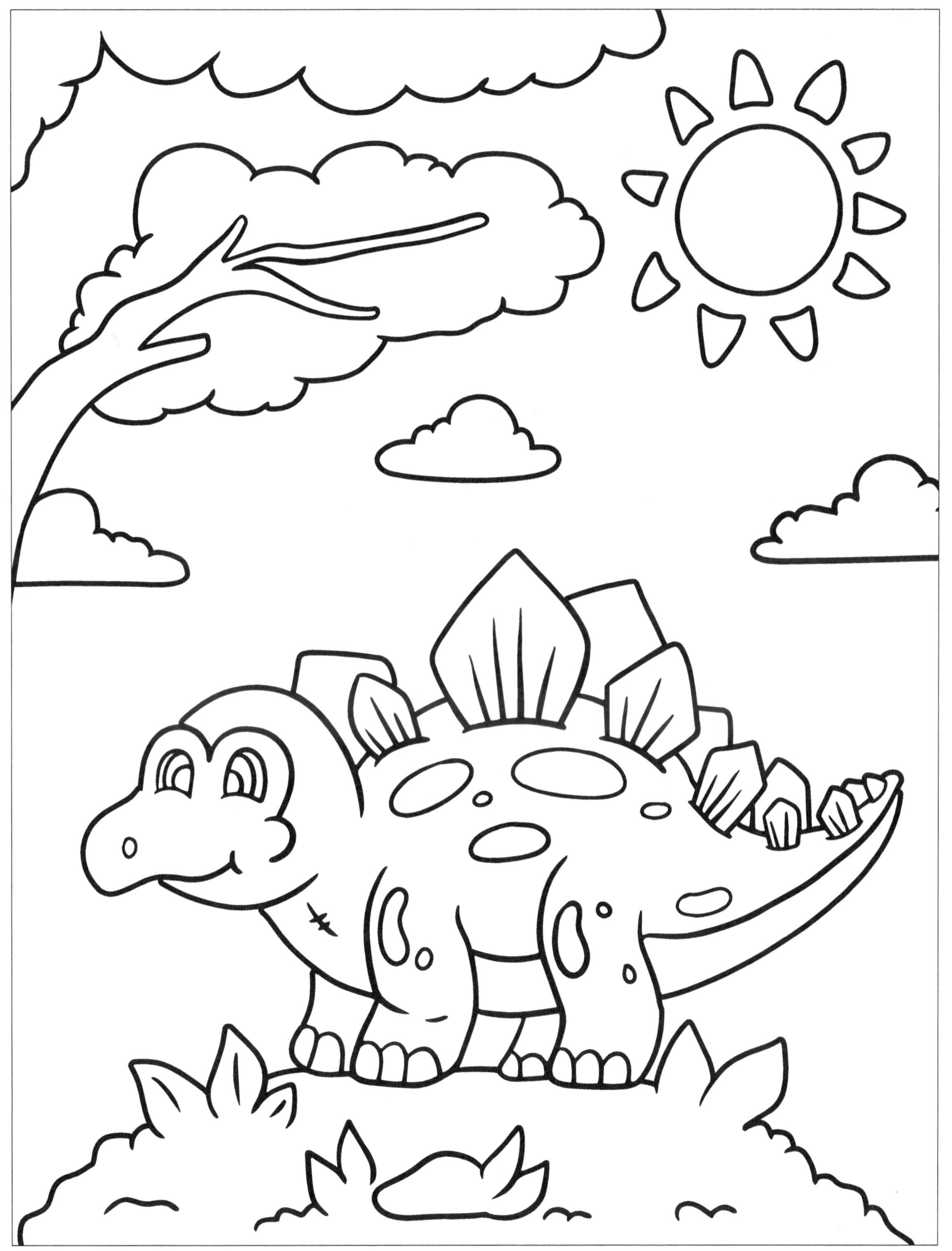

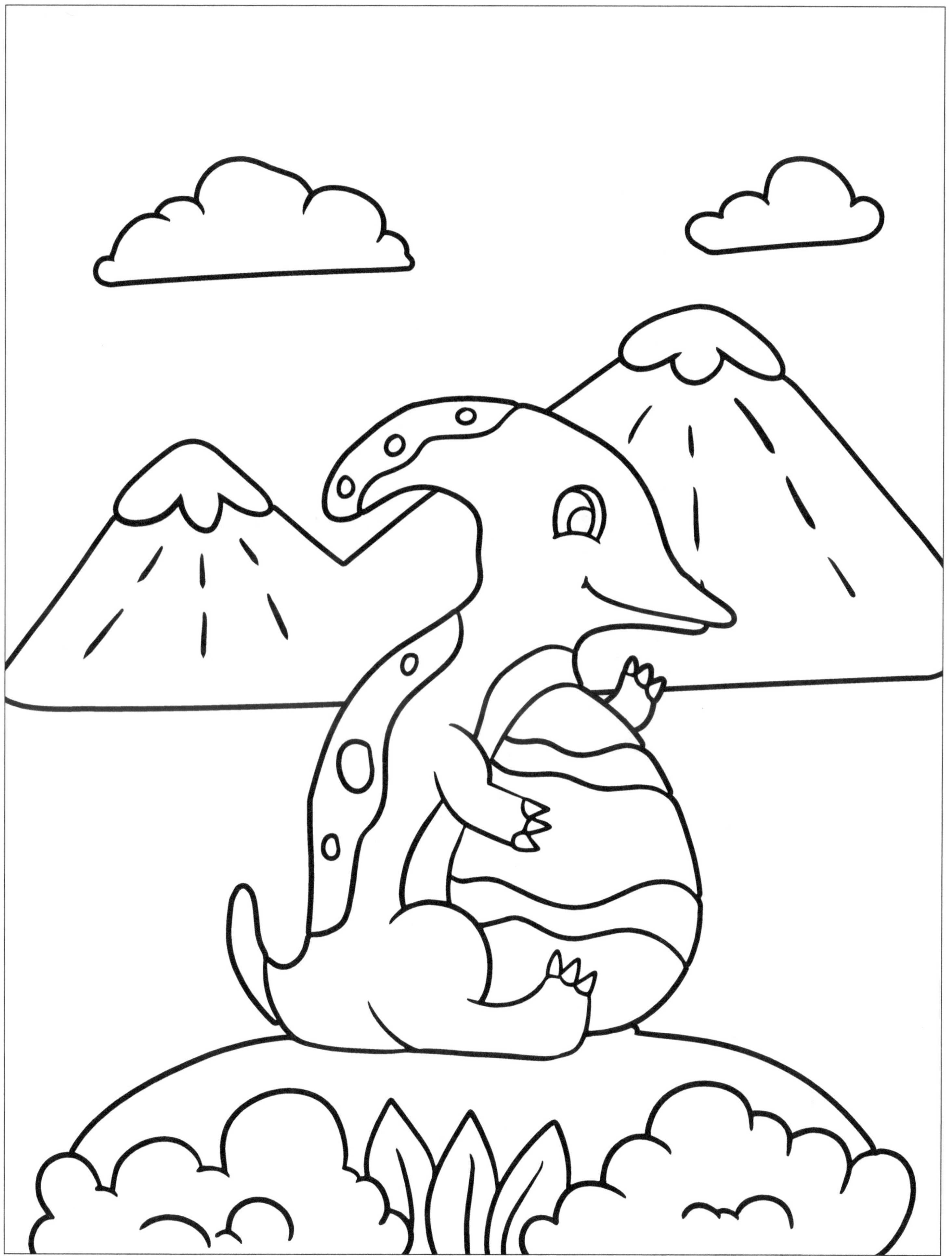

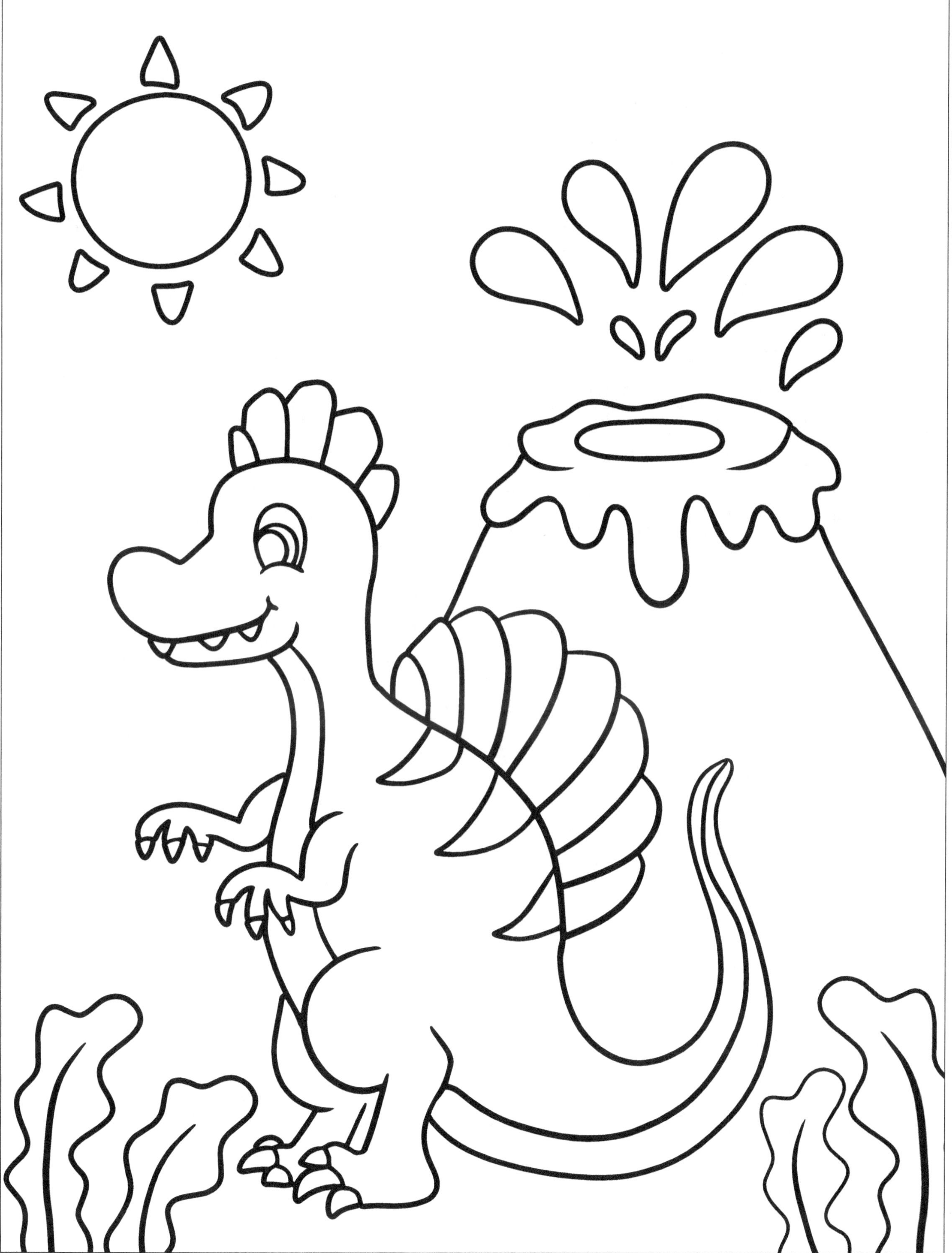

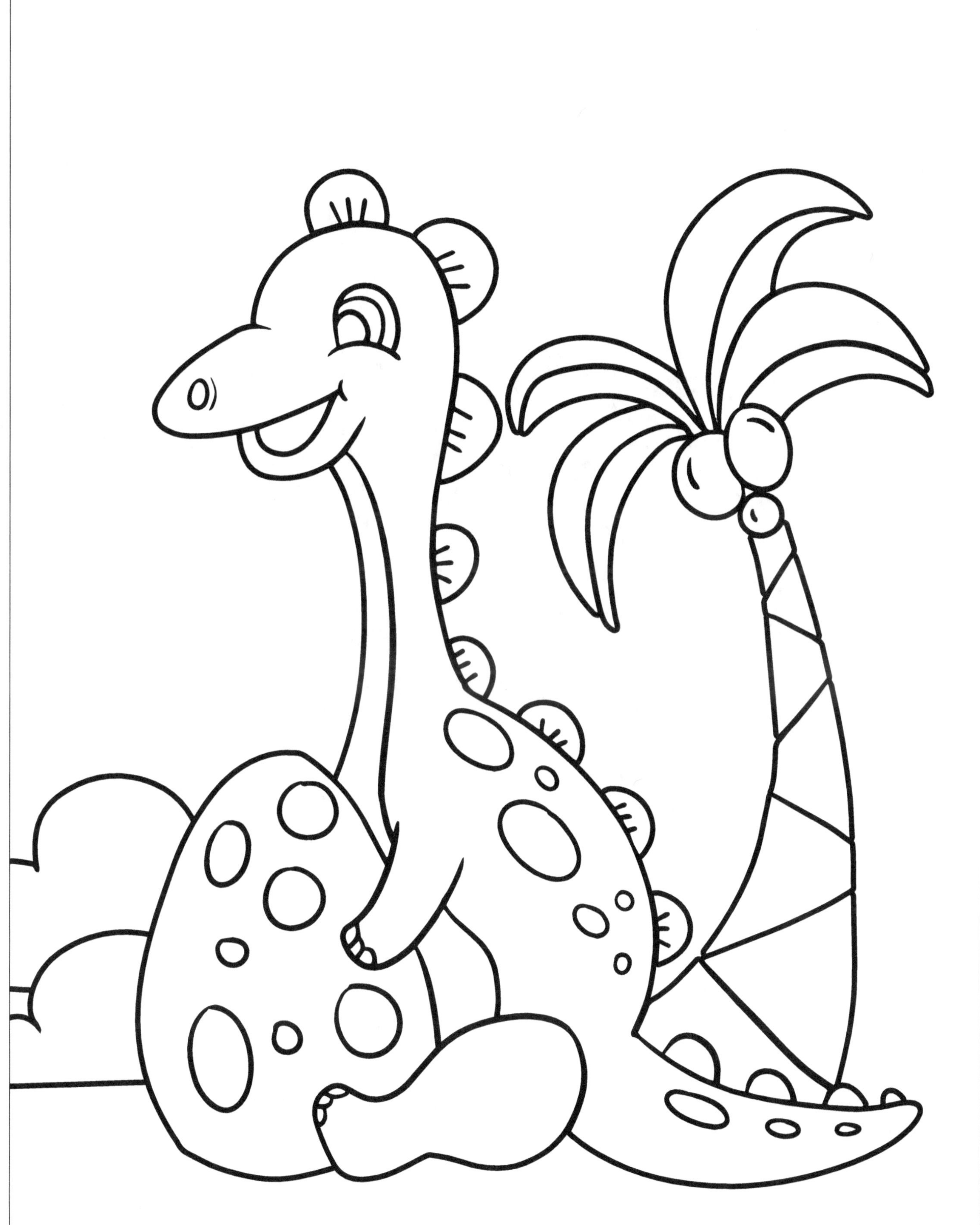

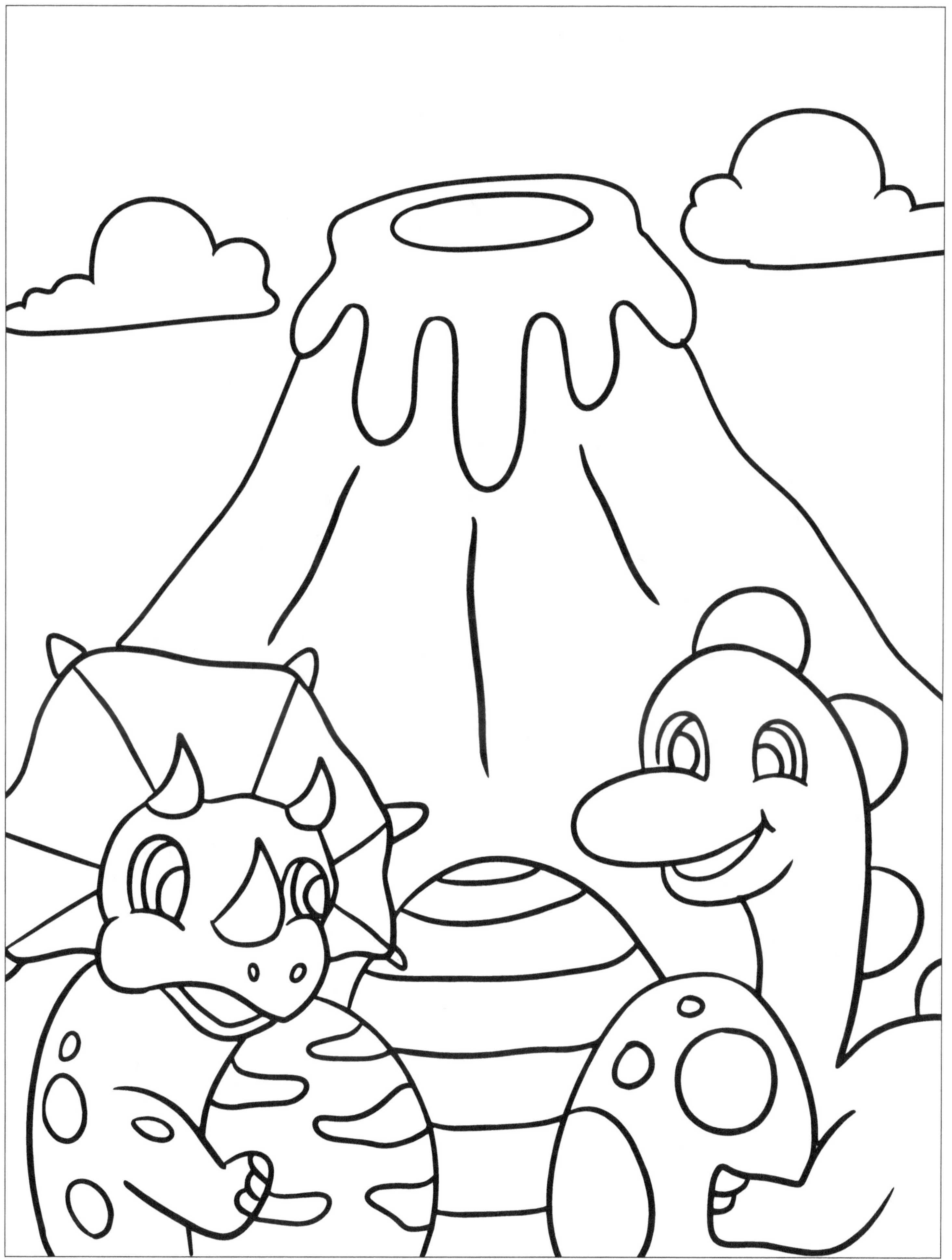

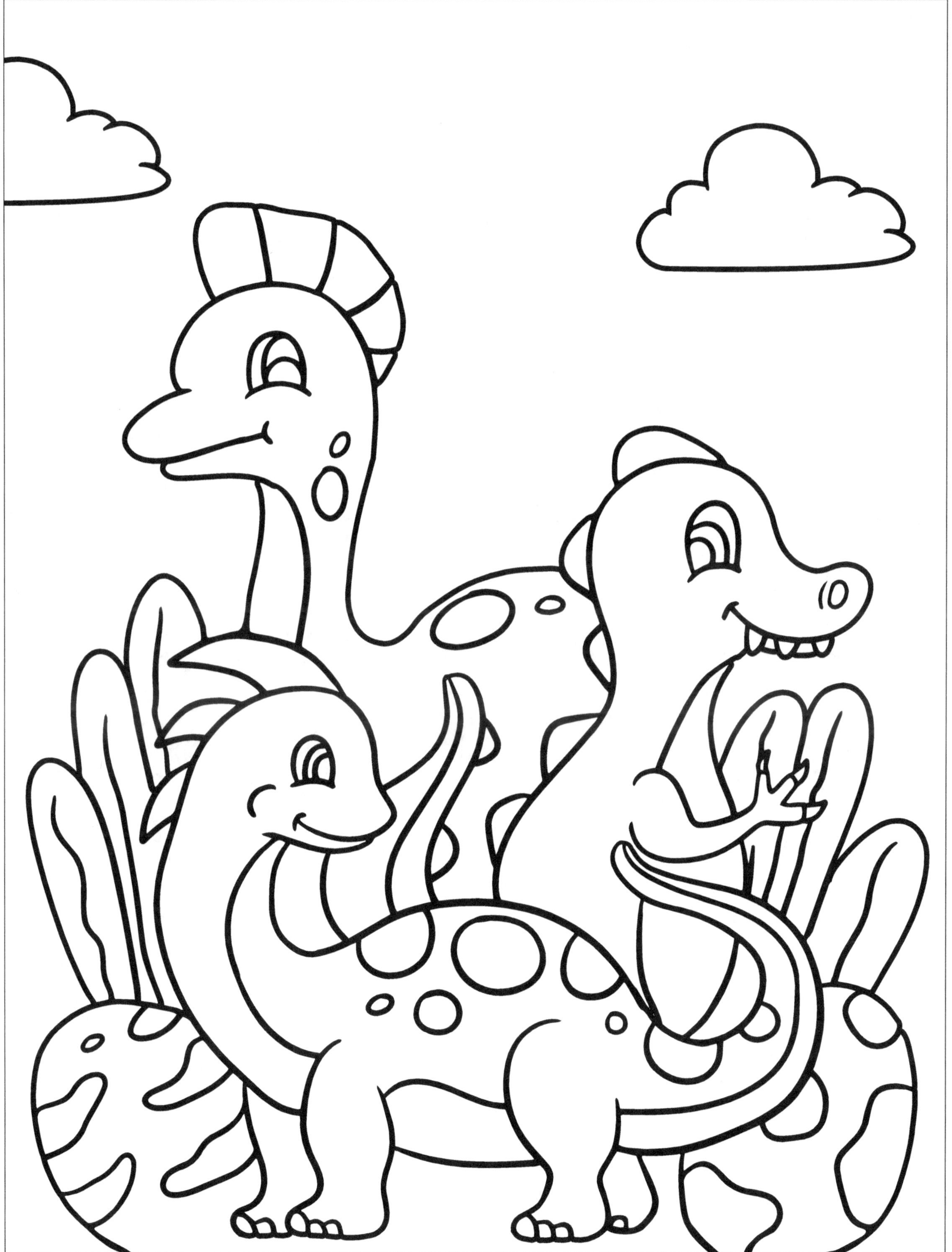

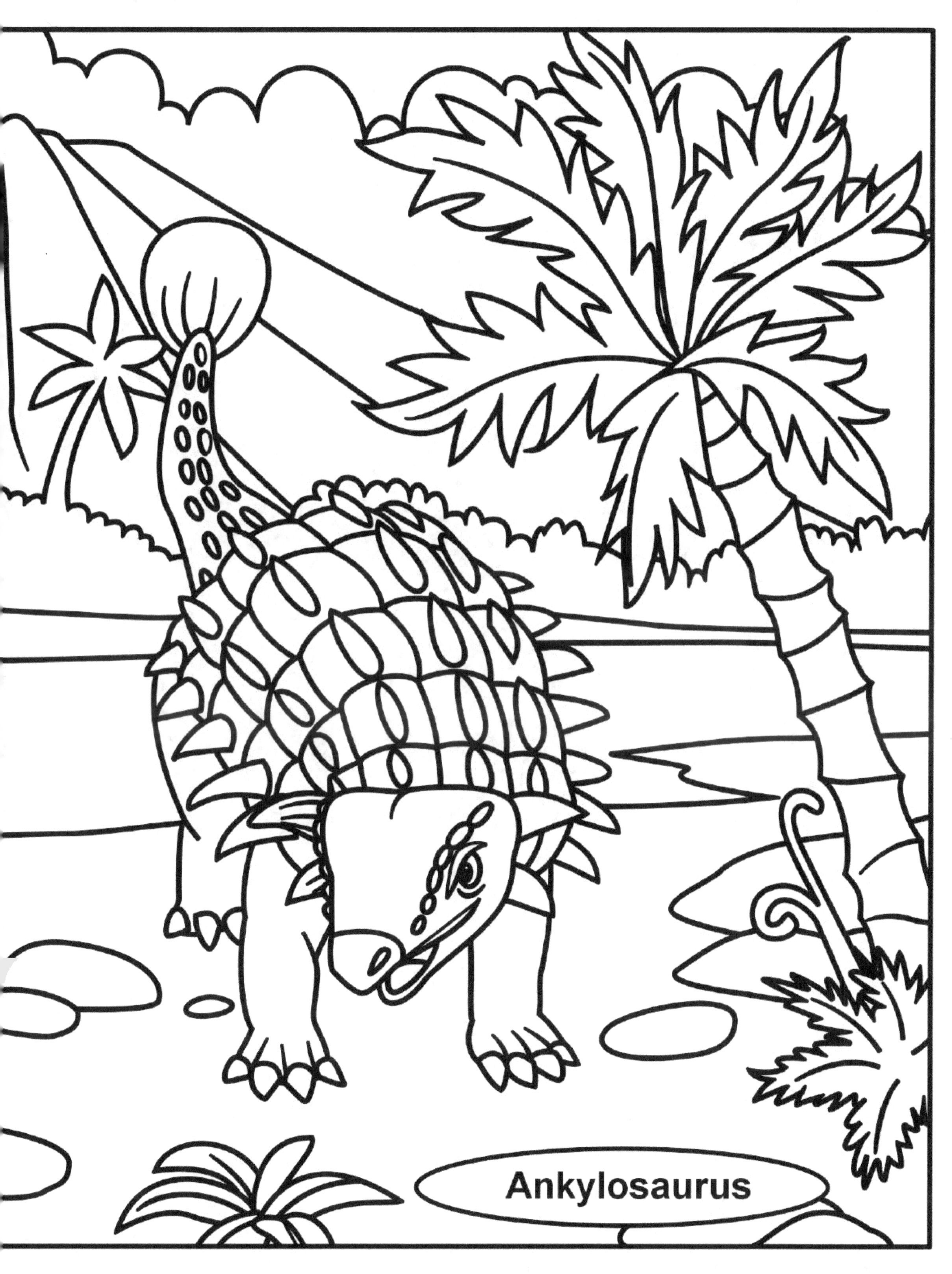
Ankylosaurus

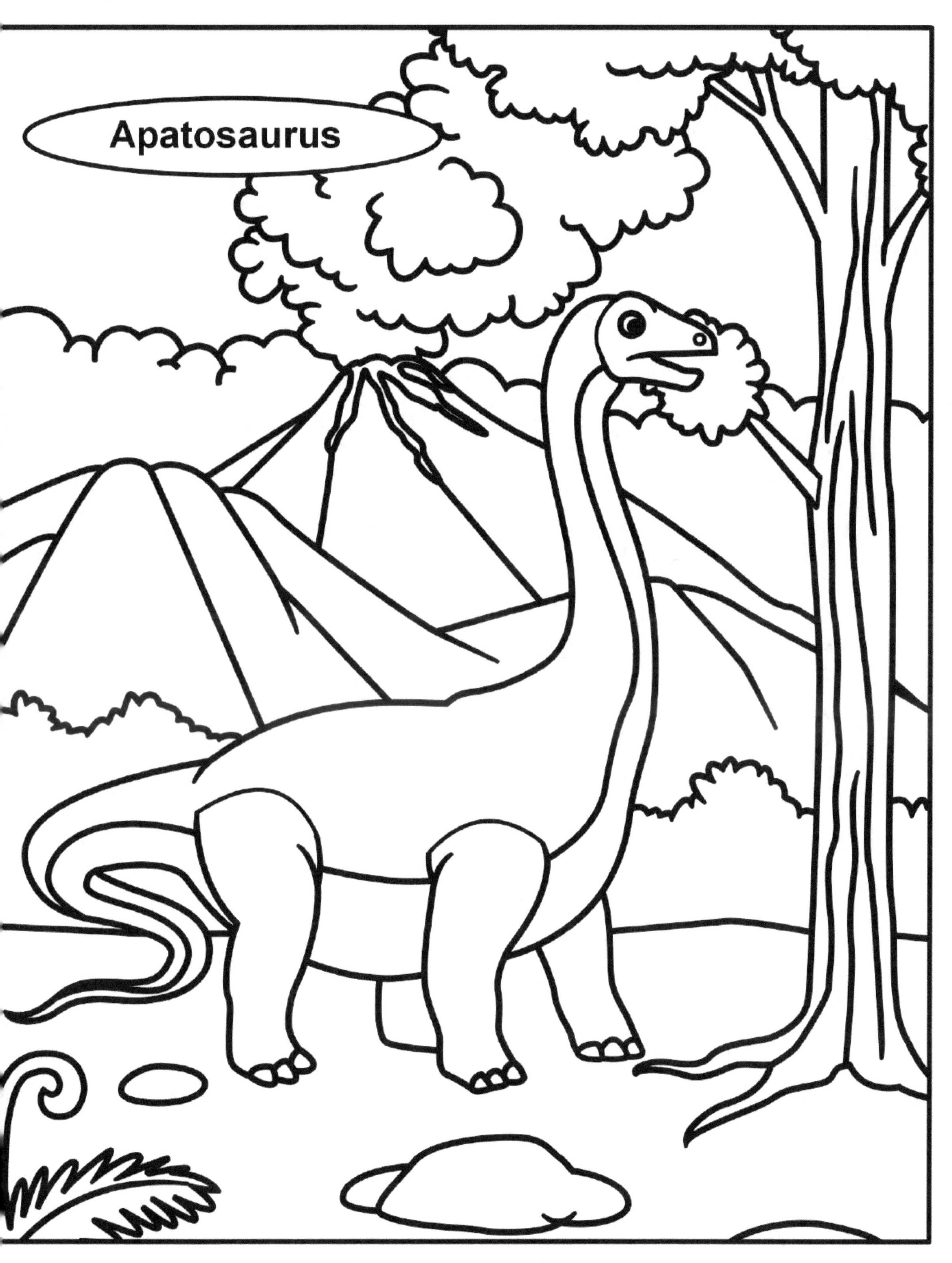
Apatosaurus

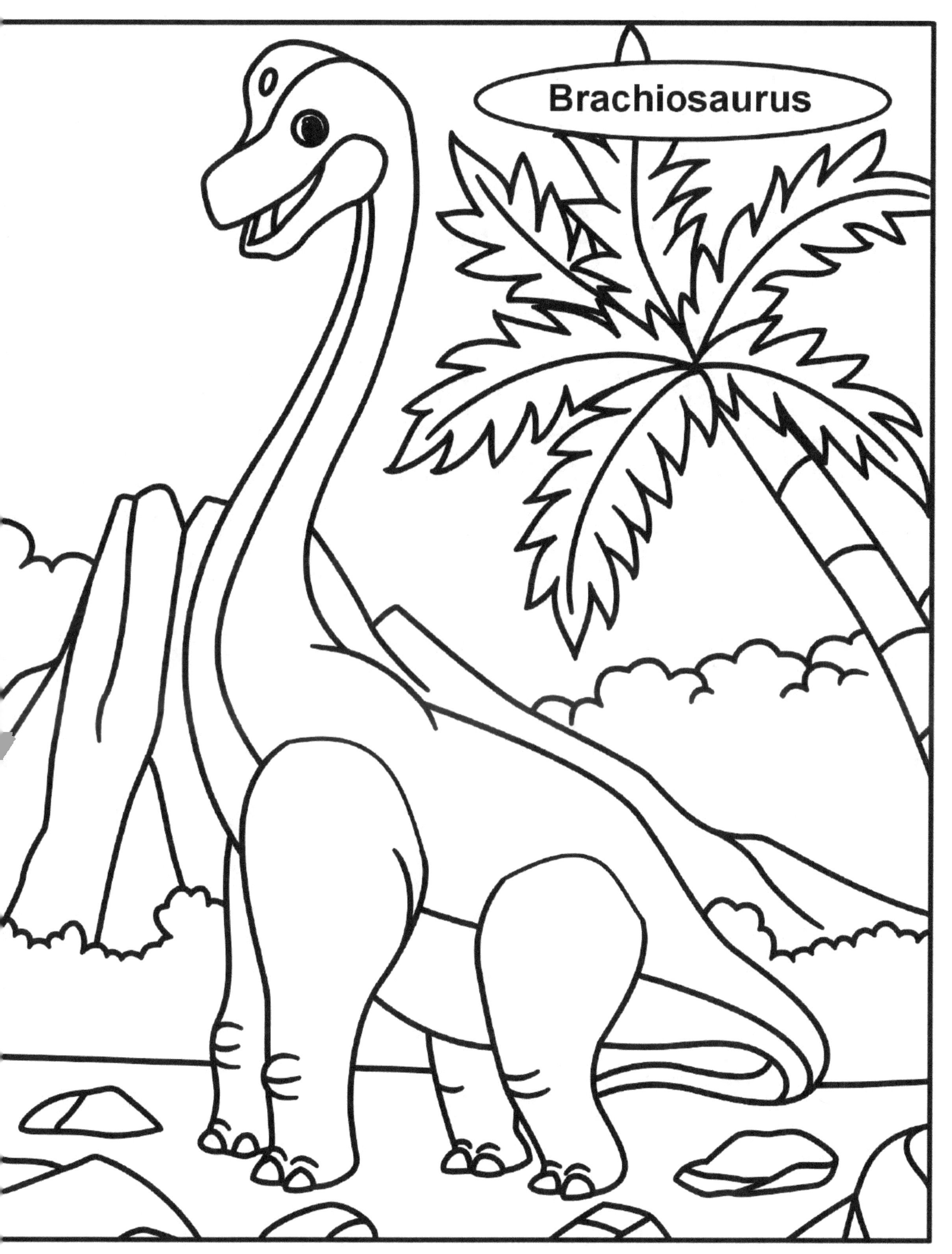
Brachiosaurus

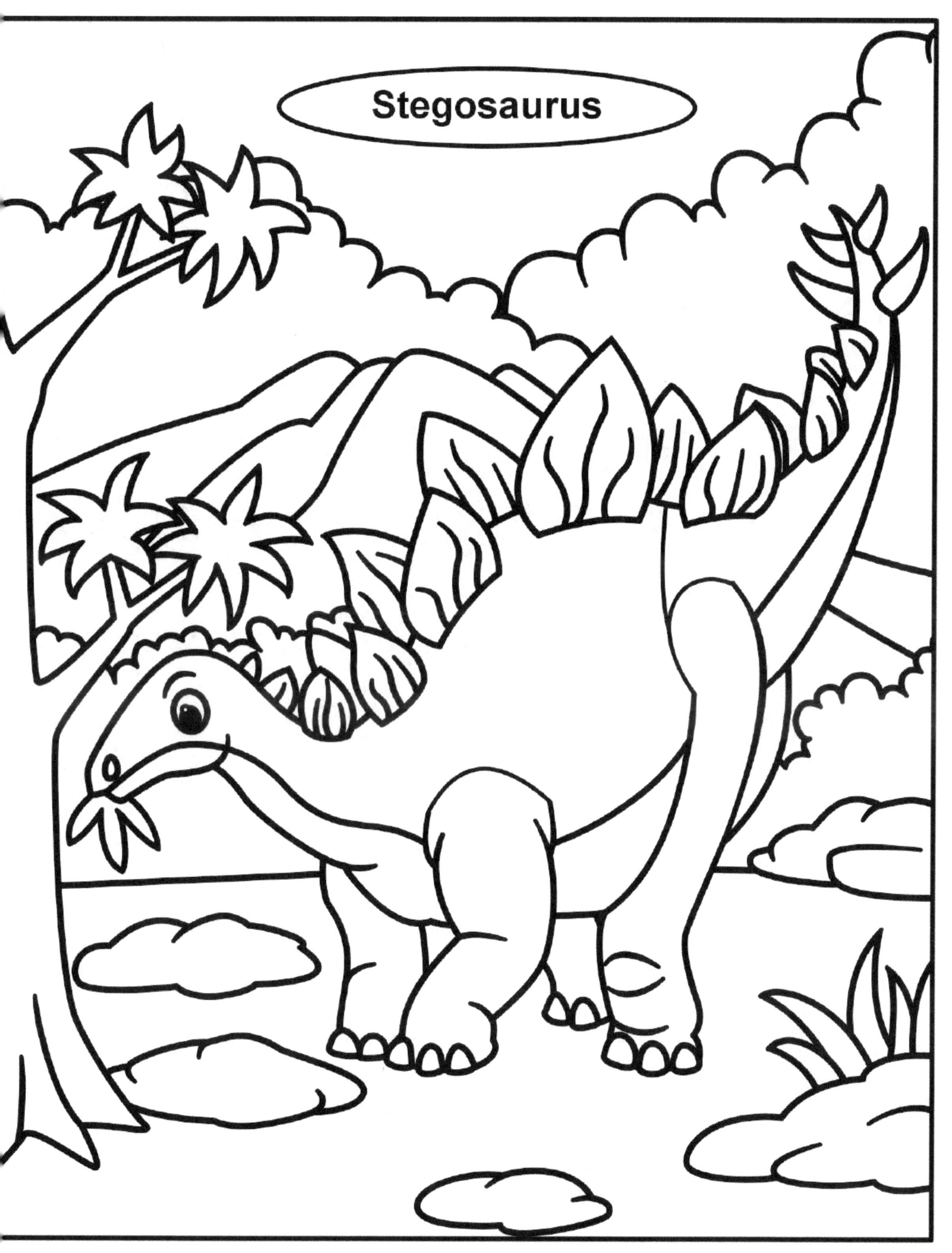
Stegosaurus

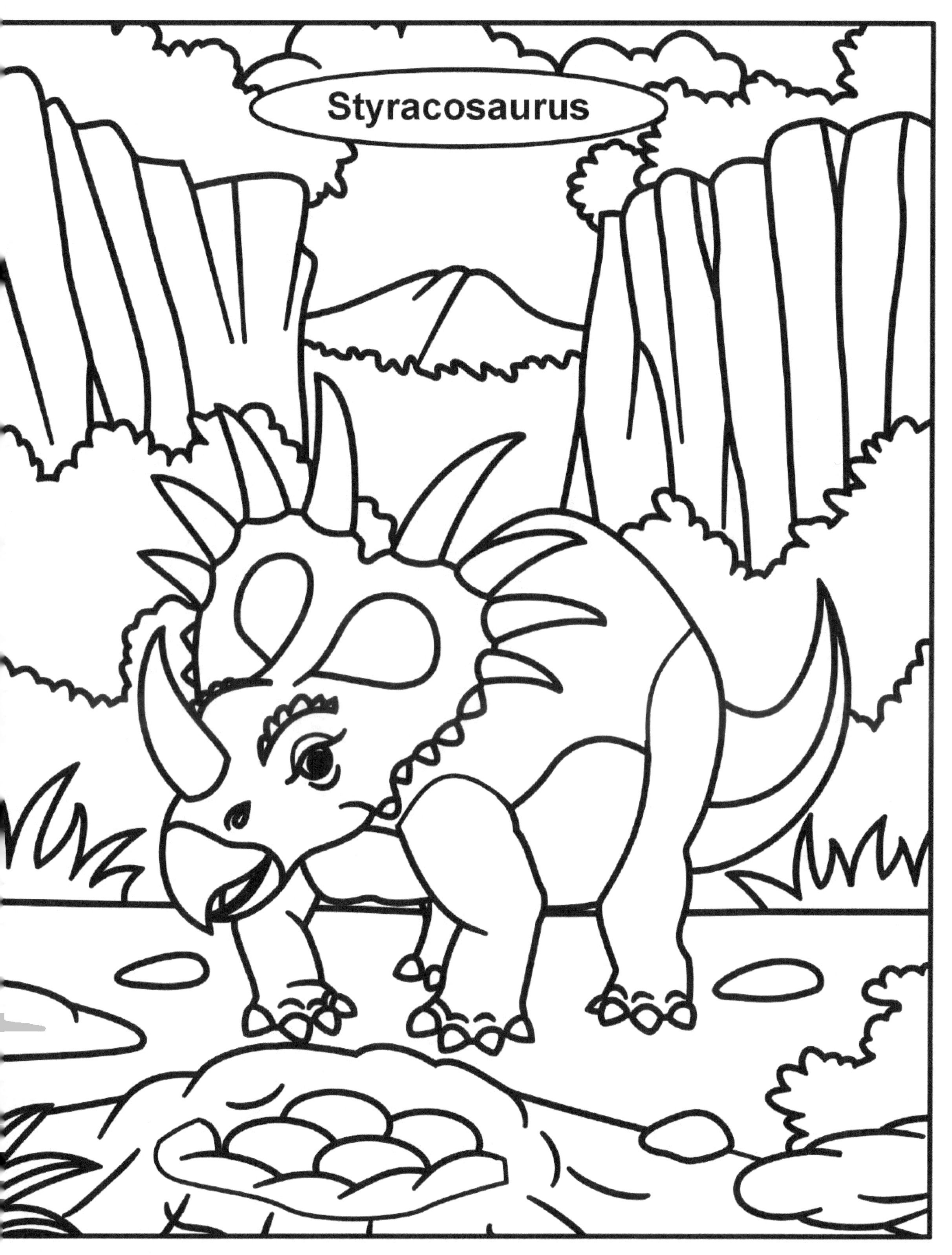
Styracosaurus

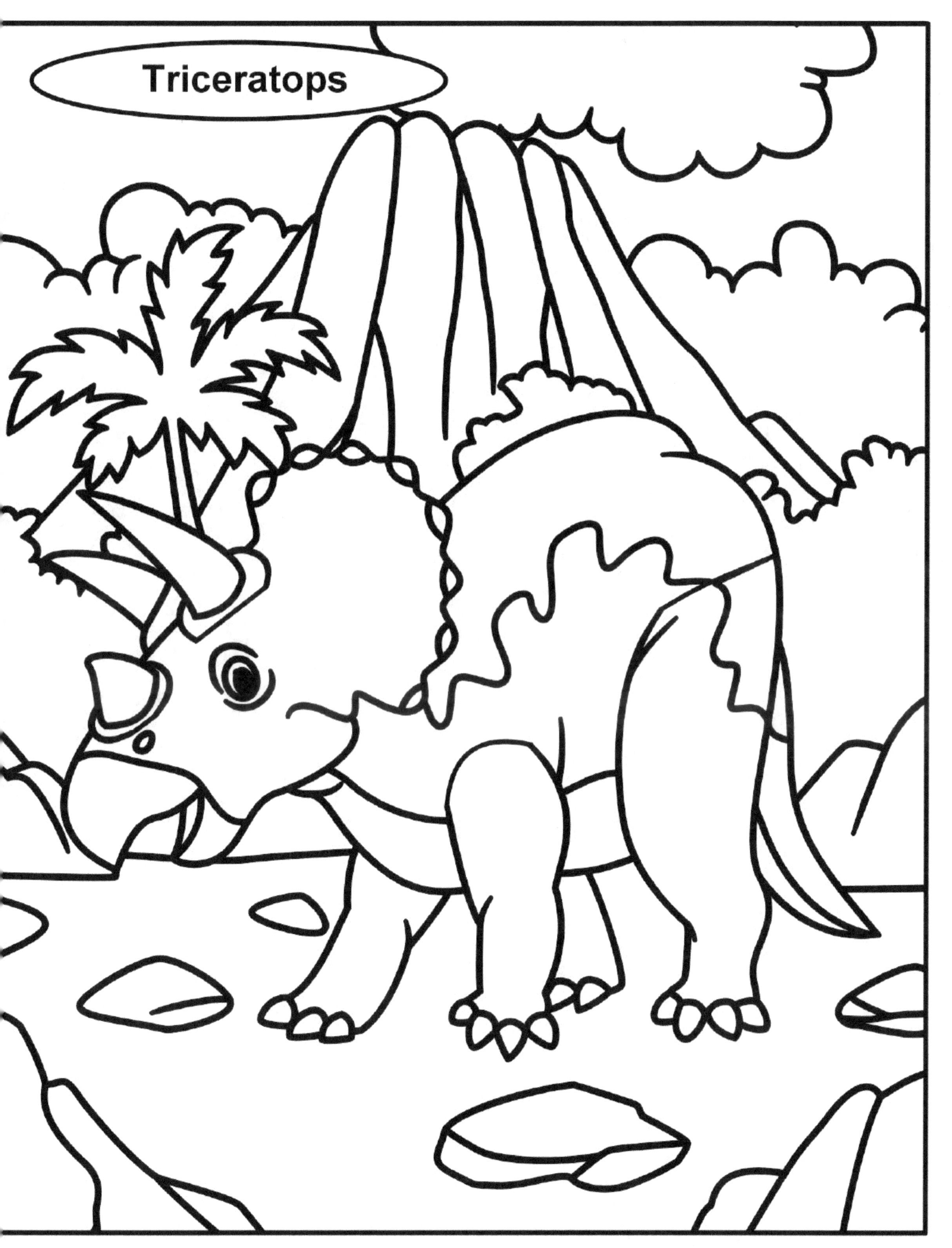

Triceratops

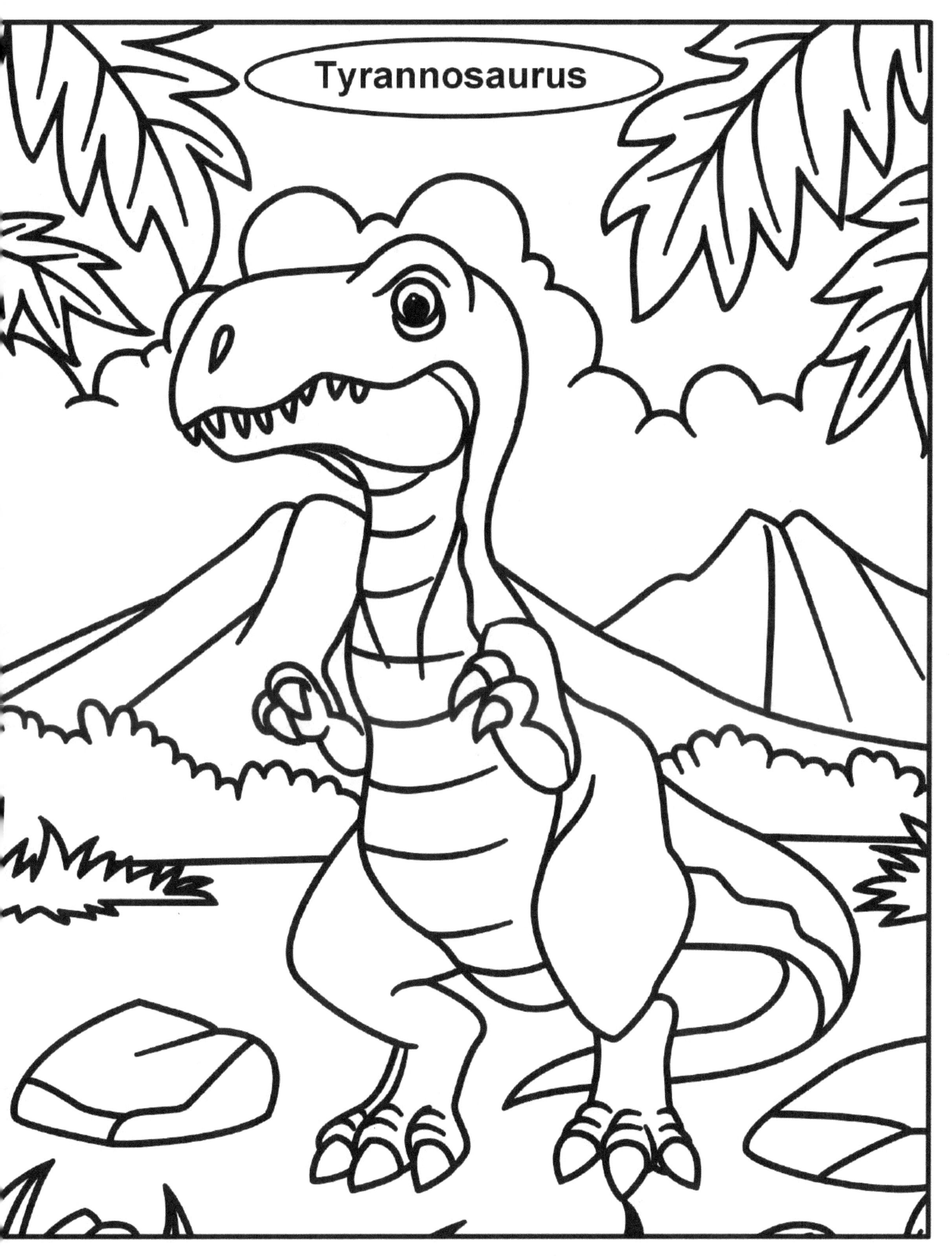
Tyrannosaurus

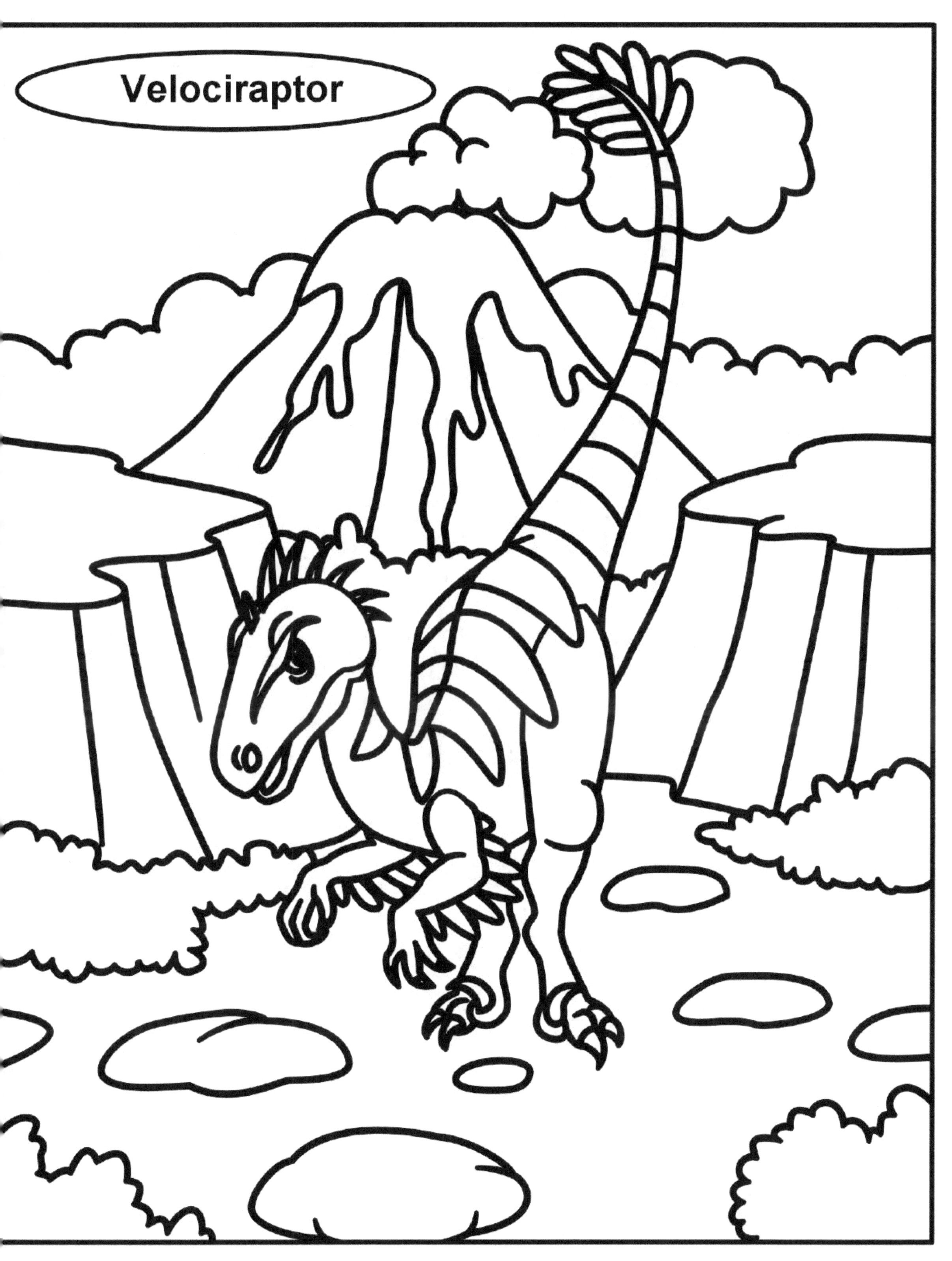
Velociraptor

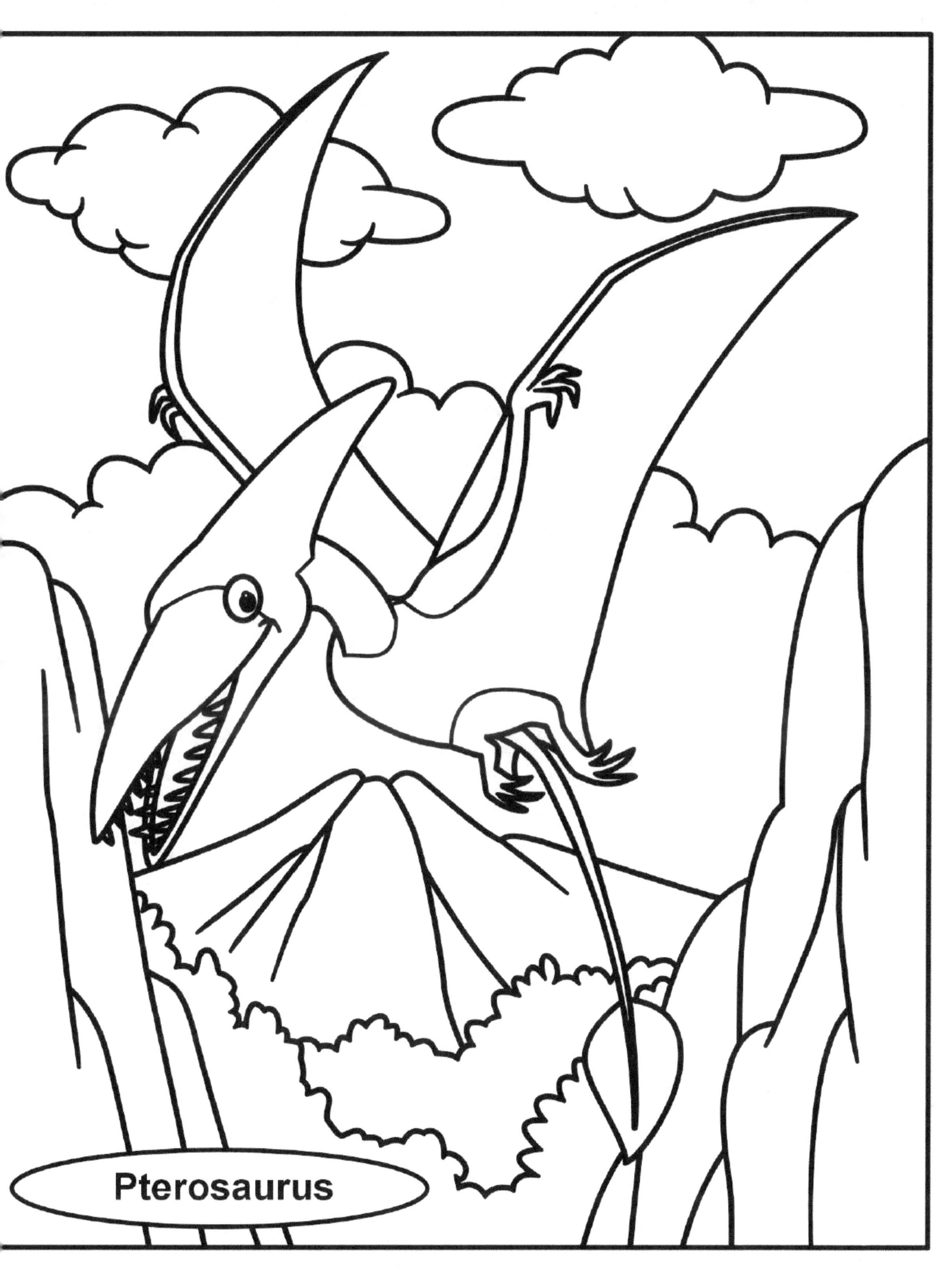
Pterosaurus

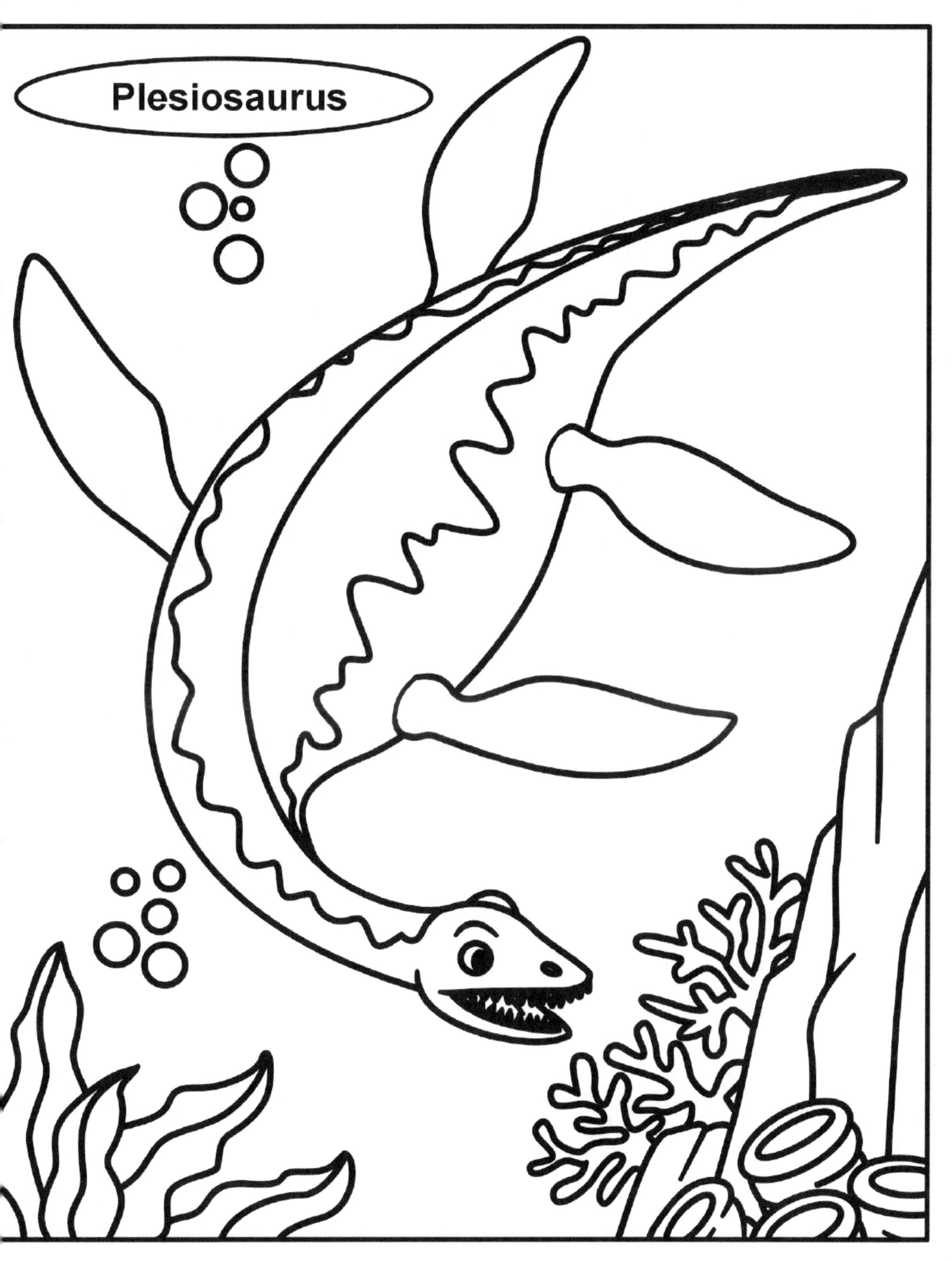
Plesiosaurus